Andreas Behr

Investment and Liquidity Constraints

nbf neue betriebswirtschaftliche forschung

(Folgende Bände sind zuletzt erschienen:)

Band 254 Dr. Thomas Ritter
Innovationserfolg durch Netzwerk-Kompetenz

Band 255 Dr. Gerhard Satzger
Kapitalintensive Leistungen im globalen Wettbewerb

Band 256 Dr. Michael Noeske
Durchlaufzeiten in Informationsprozessen

Band 257 Dr. Marcus Rodermann
Strategisches Synergiemanagement

Band 258 Dr. Dietrich von der Oelsnitz
Marktorientierter Unternehmenswandel
Strategisches Synergiemanagement

Band 259 Dr. Thorsten Blecker
Unternehmung ohne Grenzen

Band 260 Dr. Alexander Philipp Mrzyk
Ertragswertorientierte Kreditwürdigkeitsprüfung bei Existenzgründungen

Band 261 PD Dr. Michaela Haase
Institutionenökonomische Betriebswirtschaftstheorie

Band 262 Prof. Dr. Robert Neumann
Die Organisation als Ordnung des Wissens

Band 263 Prof. Dr. Norbert Klingebiel
integriertes Performance Measurement

Band 264 Prof. Dr. Insa Sjurts
Kollektive Unternehmensstrategie

Band 265 Prof. Dr. Markus Voeth
Nutzenmessung in der Kaufverhaltensforschung

Band 266 Dr. Peter Kajüter
Proaktives Kostenmanagement

Band 267 Prof. Dr. Frank Schirmer
Reorganisationsmanagement

Band 268 Prof. Dr. Sabine Fließ
Die Steuerung von Kundenintegrationsprozessen

Band 269 PD Dr. Renate Hecker
Regulierung von Unternehmensübernahmen und Konzernrecht

Band 270 Prof. Dr. Thomas Hutzschenreuter
Wachstumsstrategien

Band 271 Prof. Dr. Frank-Martin Belz
Integratives Öko-Marketing

Band 272 PD Dr. Martin Reckenfelderbäumer
Zentrale Dienstleistungsbereiche und Wettbewerbsfähigkeit

Band 273 PD Dr. Magdalena Mißler-Behr
Fuzzybasierte Controllinginstrumente

Band 274 Dr. Werner Mussnig
Dynamisches Target Costing

Band 275 Prof. Dr. Peter Buxmann
Informationsmanagement in vernetzten Unternehmen

Band 276 PD Dr. Andreas Grüner
Scorecardbasiertes Cockpit Controlling

Band 277 PD Dr. Udo Terstege
Bezugsrechte bei Kapitalerhöhungen

Band 278 PD Dr. Thomas Walter
Interaktions-Revolution im Bankmanagement

Band 279 Prof. Dr. Dr. Andreas Löffler
Ein Paradox der Portfoliotheorie und vermögensabhängige Nutzenfunktionen

Band 280 Prof. Dr. Jörg Freiling
Ressourcenorientierte Reorganisationen

Band 281 PD Dr. Ruth Stock
Der Zusammenhang zwischen Mitarbeiter- und Kundenzufriedenheit

Band 282 Prof. Dr. Thorsten Teichert
Nutzenschätzung in Conjoint-Analysen

Band 283 Prof. Dr. Dirk Holtbrügge
Postmoderne Organisationstheorie und Organisationsgestaltung

Band 284 Prof. Dr. Daniel Klapper
Wettbewerbsverhalten und Produktlinienwettbewerb

Band 285 PD Dr. Bernhard Swoboda
Dynamische Prozesse der Internationalisierung

Band 286 Prof. Dr. Wolfgang Burr
Service Engineering bei technischen Dienstleistungen

Band 287 Prof. Dr. Udo Bankhofer
Industrielles Standortmanagement

Band 288 Prof. Dr. Lutz Kaufmann
Internationales Beschaffungsmanagement

(Fortsetzung am Ende des Buches)

Andreas Behr

Investment and Liquidity Constraints

Empirical Evidence for Germany

Deutscher Universitäts-Verlag

Bibliografische Information Der Deutschen Bibliothek
Die Deutsche Bibliothek verzeichnet diese Publikation in der Deutschen Nationalbibliografie; detaillierte bibliografische Daten sind im Internet über <http://dnb.ddb.de> abrufbar.

Habilitationsschrift Universität Frankfurt a.M., 2003

1. Auflage Dezember 2003

Lektorat: Brigitte Siegel/Nicole Schweitzer

Der Deutsche Universitäts-Verlag ist ein Unternehmen von Springer Science+Business Media.
www.duv.de

Umschlaggestaltung: Regine Zimmer, Dipl.-Designerin, Frankfurt/Main

Gedruckt auf säurefreiem und chlorfrei gebleichtem Papier

ISBN-13:978-3-8244-9127-8 e-ISBN-13:978-3-322-82010-5
DOI: 10.1007/978-3-322-82010-5

Preface

During the last decade exploring the link between financial factors and investment has become a major field of theoretical and empirical publications. Firms in a weak financial position cannot raise capital at conditions that allow financing all profitable investment projects. Some empirical findings indicate that young, fast growing, low dividend paying firms face more liquidity constraints compared to other firms and therefore exhibit stronger reactions in investment to changes of their internal financial flow. If the credit conditions of firms will be influenced through expansionary or rather restrictive monetary conditions the cycle of real activity might be accelerated through these monetary conditions and the final effects might exceed the pure effects of the interest channel alone.

In the analysis in hand the role of financial factors in the firm's investment decision is explored within the framework of the *Q*-theory of investment. The *Q*-theory is applied to a large database of German firms, covering balance sheet data for 2,314 German firms, thereof 1,342 manufacturing firms. This database, the Deutsche Bundesbank's Corporate Balance Sheet Statistics, gives the unique opportunity to analyze heterogeneity at the firm level, which is not possible using macro- or mesoeconomic data. Access to this data base was made possible during a stay at a visiting researcher in the research department at the Deutsche Bundesbank in 2002. I would like to thank Heinz Herrmann for his support and the fruitful discussions of questions arising during the research project.

I want to thank Egon Bellgardt for the many research projects carried out jointly and his always helpful advice. Finally I want to thank Werner Neubauer, Ulrich Rendtel and Roland Eisen for reading the manuscript and helpful discussions.

Andreas Behr

Contents

List of figures

List of Tables

1. Introduction

The aim of this analysis is to explore the role of financial factors in the firm's investment decision within the framework of the *Q*-theory of investment. The *Q*-theory we apply to a large database of German firms, covering balance sheet data for 2,314 German firms, thereof 1,342 manufacturing firms. This database, the Deutsche Bundesbank's Corporate Balance Sheet Statistics, gives the unique opportunity to analyze heterogeneity at the firm level, which is not possible using macro- or mesoeconomic data.

Tobin's *Q* plays a dominant role in empirical research on investment behavior and can be seen as one of the standard approaches. *Q* models of investment are attractive in several respects. Theoretically the *Q*-model can be derived explicitly from an optimization problem, which the firm faces when deciding about new investments.[1] Under quite strong assumptions a linear relationship between the ratio of investment to the capital stock and a measure of *Q* can be derived. Theoretically *Q* is a sufficient statistic for determining the investment decision if the capital market is perfect.[2]

During the last decade exploring the link between financial factors and investment has become a major field of theoretical and empirical publications. While in the neoclassical framework there is a dichotomy between real investment and the financing issues due to the assumption of perfect capital markets, this dichotomy is increasingly questioned in recent published papers. The neoclassical theorem of Modigliani and Miller stating the independence of real and financial decisions is rejected by a now large number of studies finding significant links between liquidity and investment. The famous paper by Fazzari, Hubbard and Petersen published 1988 can be seen as the starting point of the still ongoing fruitful research on the links between liquidity and investment. According to their findings firms in a weak financial position cannot raise capital at conditions that allow financing all profitable investment projects. If the credit conditions of firms will be influenced through expansionary or rather restrictive monetary conditions the cycle

---

1 In the following we use the upper case symbol *Q* throughout the text indicating all different measures, whether they are based on share prices or on values gained by direct forecasting systems.

2 But see Caballero/Leahy (1996) for the case of fixed costs of capital stock adjustment.

of real activity might be accelerated through these monetary conditions and the final effects might exceed the pure effects of the interest channel alone.

There is now an amount of empirical literature accumulated strengthening the assumption of existing liquidity constraints. In their influential analysis Fazzari/-Hubbard/Petersen (1988) found a significant higher influence of cash flow on investment for firms a priori classified as liquidity constraint. Other papers e.g. Hoshi/-Kashyab/Scharfstein (1991), Hubbard/Kashyab/Whited (1995) and Hu/Schiantarelli (1998) using similar approaches confirmed this result for different countries and different time periods.

These empirical findings indicate that some firms are influenced by their state of liquidity different compared to other firms. It is assumed that young, fast growing, low dividend paying firms face more liquidity constraints compared to other firms and therefore exhibit stronger reactions in investment to changes of their internal financial flow.

These empirical findings can plausibly be interpreted in the context of agency costs arising from information asymmetries (Myers and Majluf, 1984) and contract enforcement problems (Jensen and Meckling, 1986).

Because all the relevant information determining the investment decision should be included in Q, additional variables like cash flow or sales should not improve the explanatory power of the investment equation. In spite of this theoretical argument empirically there is overwhelming evidence that using further variables beside Tobin's Q in the investment equation improves the explanatory power considerably.[3]

There are two possible and competing explanations for the additional variable's significance, especially liquidity measures and sales. One reason might be that the operationalisation of Tobin's Q is rather unsatisfactory and the resulting measurement error can lead to low explanatory power of Tobin's Q itself and to significant coefficients of other explanatory variables.[4] Another reason for these empirical findings might be seen in imperfections in the capital markets. If firms are liquidity constrained

---

3 See e.g. the overview article by Chirinko (1993).

4 See Chirinko (1993), S. 1889 and Erickson/Whited (2000a) for a discussion of the measurement problems and related econometric problems.

because of capital market imperfections the firms might respond to an increase in cash flow with an increase in investment spending even if it is controlled for investment opportunities through *Q*.[5]

Therefore, at this state of research, two critical problems remain. First the question remains whether due to operationalisation problems *Q* does not contain all information relevant for the investment decision. In this case, even without any financial factors influencing the investment decision, cash flow or sales measures can show up significant solely because they might contain information about future profitability of investment projects. Second, several empirical studies divide the sample into classes of more and less severe liquidity constrained firms and find stronger reaction to liquidity for firms a priori classified as constrained. The question arises how sensitive the empirical findings are to the chosen indicators of financial constraintness. The results on its own only allow the conclusion that smaller or faster growing firms or lower dividend paying firms react stronger to cash flow compared to other firms. The conclusion often drawn, that this result indicates severe capital market imperfections rests heavily on further assumptions. And these assumptions, necessary to draw far-reaching conclusions from the empirical evidence, Kaplan/Zingales (1997, 2000) questioned forcefully. Kaplan and Zingales doubt the validity of the empirical findings in several ways. First they assume a „publication selection bias“, second by re-analyzing the data used originally by Fazzari/Kashyap/Petersen they find a high sensitivity of the results concerning the chosen liquidity measure and third they doubt the assumed monotonic relation between liquidity constraints and the sensitivity of investment to liquidity.[6]

In this analysis we explore the role of cash flow on investment in different ways. First we use a complex procedure to calculate reliable replacement values of the firm's capital stock[7] and a vector autoregressive approach (VAR) for panel data to estimate present values of the future profitabilities of capital to calculate *Q*. This direct forecasting approach, as Chirinko (1993) named it, is based on a VAR forecasting model and was first suggested by Abel and Blanchard (1986) for aggregate times series.

---

5 See Hubbard (1998) for an overview of the issue of financial constraints and investment behavior.

6 See Kaplan/Zingales (1997), p. 170. See also the discussion in Kaplan/Zingales (2000) and Fazzari/Hubbard/Petersen (2000).

7 See Hayashi (1997) for a discussion of the biases resulting from the use on non-adequate measures of the capital stock.

This approach in the context of the *Q*-theory was extended by Gilchrist and Himmelberg (1995, 1998) for panel data. The achievement of this direct forecasting approach is the applicability of the *Q*-theory to non-quoted firms as well. Second, by a priori grouping of firms which are more likely to face financial constraints and therefore are expected to show higher cash flow sensitivity, we test the hypothesis of the existence of capital constraints in Germany.

The following section briefly discusses the *Q*-theory of investment, including the assumption introduced to derive estimable linear investment functions, and the theoretical link between internal net wealth and the investment decision of the firm. Information costs and the need for costly monitoring are seen as a possible source that could create a wedge between the costs of external and internal finance, which could result in a direct link between changes in net wealth and investment.

Since the consideration of adjustment costs results in the inclusion of lagged endogenous variables in the investment equation, we have to apply dynamic panel data estimation techniques. Chapter three gives an overview of suggested panel data estimators and analyses their empirical performance in a Monte Carlo study. Since the this chapter inevitable is rather technical, the reader interested mainly in the economic issues, might proceed with chapter four.

In chapter four we discuss in depth the measurement problems when applying the *Q*-theory of investment to firm level balance sheet data. The two variables being subject to most measurement problems are the capital stock at replacement values, which are not available in the data set and has to be estimated, as well as the central variable *Q* itself. The two problems are overcome via applying a new algorithm including sectoral corrections to available historical cost data of the capital stock and a vector autoregressive forecasting procedure to derive proxies for *Q*.

Chapter five contains the empirical results. Our main object of interest is the estimation of *Q*-investment functions including measures of changes in net wealth to assess the impact of these changes on the firm's investment. Since the data base facilitates disaggregated analysis, we explore, beside in an aggregate analysis, the investment behavior for different groups of firms according to size and sectors.

Chapter six summarizes our findings.

2. The *Q*-theory of investment and the role of internal funds

The *Q*-theory of investment can be said to be the standard approach to explain investment behavior. The *Q*-theory is microeconomic in nature and derives an equilibrium solution to the firm's investment problem explicitly from the firm's optimization problem.

The economic models of business fixed investment can broadly be classified into two classes of models. Both explain the optimal level of the firm's capital stock from the solution of the profit maximization problem. But where the first and mostly former class of models (an overview is given in Jorgensen 1971) do not explain the optimal path of adjustment of the actual capital stock to the optimal one, the second class of models explicitly derive the optimal evolution of the capital stock from the underlying optimization problem. The difference therefore can be seen in the step from the static problem of optimal factor demand to dynamic investment models. This step can either be done by ad hoc specifications or by an explicit derivation of the adjustment path in the newer class of investment models.

The gain of course is achieved by making strong assumptions about the cost of adjustment when the level of the capital stock is changed. The strong assumptions are necessary to rationalize the observed slow adjustment of the capital stock. Usually the cost of adjustment is assumed to be strictly convex in the amount of investment what implies increasing marginal costs. Therefore deviations between the actual and the optimal capital stock will be reduced through a sequence of smaller investments rather then through a one time large change of the capital stock. The cost of adjustment can be thought of installation costs or costs caused by the disruptions of the production process when new investment is undertaken.

In the following the *Q* model, as a representative of the models explicitly referring to adjustment costs, will be illustrated.

2.1. The *Q*-Model

In the following we assume the firm to maximize the discounted stream of future profits.[1] To abstract from agency problems, it is further assumed that the management, which at the same time holds all equity, makes the decisions of the firm. Hence profit maximizing leads to the same behavior of the firm as maximizing the value of equity. The profit-maximizing problem can be formulated as follows:[2]

$$V_t = E\left[\sum_{j=0}^{\infty} \beta_{t+j} \Pi_{t+j} \mid \Omega_t\right]$$

The firm is assumed to maximize the expected value of the sum of the discounted net cash flow Π_t given the state of information Ω_t at time t. The discount factor between period t and period $t+j$ is denoted by β_{t+j} and is assumed to be the product of the single period discount rates:

$$\beta_{t+j} = \prod_{i=1}^{j} \left(1 + r_{t+i}\right)^{-1}, j = 1, 2, 3, \ldots, \infty.$$

The net cash flow Π_t is the difference between sales and costs of production:

$$\Pi_t = p_t F(K_t, L_t) - w_t L_t - p_t G(I_t, K_t) - p_t^I I_t$$

The output is given by the amount of production F, given the capital stock K_t and the other factors of production, mainly labor, L_t that are assumed to be adjusted instantaneously minus the lost output G caused by adjusting the capital stock. The function of adjustment cost G is assumed to be strictly convex in investment and to be additively separable from the gross production function.

In the simplest case, where the firm is financed through shares only, the difference between dividends D_t and new shares issued N_t in period t equals the firm's profit:

$$\Pi_t = D_t - N_t$$

---

1 The following representation is based on the papers by Blundell/Bond/Meghir (1995), Blundell et. al. (1992) and Hayashi (1982).

2 We drop the index i for individual firms to ease readability.

If asset markets are efficient, that assets are valued at the expected present value of the associated income streams, then V_t is the stock market value of the firm.

According to the capital accumulation constraint the beginning of period t capital stock equals the beginning of period t-1 capital stock less depreciation plus period t gross investment. If it is assumed that investment takes place at the beginning of the year and is productive immediately, we have the following accumulation constraint:

$$K_t = (1-\delta)K_{t-1} + I_t$$

The maximization problem the firm faces can be expressed as a dynamic programming problem:

$$V_t(K_{t-1}) = \left\{ \max_{L_t, I_t} \Pi(K_t, L_t, I_t) + E[\beta_{t+1} V_{t+1}(K_t) \mid \Omega_t] \right\}$$

Inserting the accumulation constraint yields

$$V_t(K_{t-1}) = \left\{ \max_{L_t, I_t} \Pi((1-\delta)K_{t-1} + I_t, L_t, I_t) + E[\beta_{t+1} V_{t+1}(K_t) \mid \Omega_t] \right\}$$

To find the maximum, the function is differentiated with respect to K_{t-1} and I_t to get the first order conditions.

The first order condition for investment I_t:

$$\frac{\partial V_t(K_{t-1})}{\partial I_t} = \frac{\partial \left\{ \max_{L_t, I_t} \Pi((1-\delta)K_{t-1} + I_t, L_t, I_t) + E[\beta_{t+1} V_{t+1}(K_t) \mid \Omega_t] \right\}}{\partial I_t} = 0$$

$$= \frac{\partial \Pi((1-\delta)K_{t-1} + I_t, L_t, I_t)}{\partial I_t} + \frac{\partial E[\beta_{t+1} V_{t+1}(K_t) \mid \Omega_t]}{\partial I_t}$$

$$= \frac{\partial \Pi_t}{\partial I_t} + \frac{\partial \Pi_t}{\partial K_t}\frac{\partial K_t}{\partial I_t} + E\left[\beta_{t+1}\frac{\partial V_{t+1}}{\partial K_t}\frac{\partial K_t}{\partial I_t} \mid \Omega_t\right]$$

$$= \frac{\partial \Pi_t}{\partial I_t} + \frac{\partial \Pi_t}{\partial K_t} + E\left[\beta_{t+1}\frac{\partial V_{t+1}}{\partial K_t} \mid \Omega_t\right] = 0$$

The first order condition for the capital stock in the previous period K_{t-1}:

$$\frac{\partial V_t(K_{t-1})}{\partial K_{t-1}} = \frac{\partial \left\{ \max\limits_{L_t, I_t} \Pi((1-\delta)K_{t-1} + I_t, L_t, I_t) + E[\beta_{t+1} V_{t+1}(K_t) \mid \Omega_t] \right\}}{\partial K_{t-1}} = 0$$

$$\frac{\partial V_t(K_{t-1})}{\partial K_{t-1}} = \frac{\partial \Pi((1-\delta)K_{t-1} + I_t, L_t, I_t)}{\partial K_{t-1}} + \frac{\partial E[\beta_{t+1} V_{t+1}(K_t) \mid \Omega_t]}{\partial K_{t-1}}$$

$$= \frac{\partial V_t(K_{t-1})}{\partial K_{t-1}} = \frac{\partial \Pi_t}{\partial K_t}\frac{\partial K_t}{\partial K_{t-1}} + E\left[\beta_{t+1}\frac{\partial V_{t+1}}{\partial K_t}\frac{\partial K_t}{\partial K_{t-1}} \mid \Omega_t\right] = 0$$

$$= (1-\delta)\frac{\partial \Pi_t}{\partial K_t} + (1-\delta)E\left[\beta_{t+1}\frac{\partial V_{t+1}}{\partial K_t} \mid \Omega_t\right] = 0$$

Using the first order condition for investment

$$\frac{\partial V_t(K_{t-1})}{\partial I_t} = \frac{\partial \Pi_t}{\partial I_t} + \frac{\partial \Pi_t}{\partial K_t} + E\left[\beta_{t+1}\frac{\partial V_{t+1}}{\partial K_t} \mid \Omega_t\right] = 0$$

$$(1-\delta)E\left[\beta_{t+1}\frac{\partial V_{t+1}}{\partial K_t} \mid \Omega_t\right] = -(1-\delta)\frac{\partial \Pi_t}{\partial I_t} - (1-\delta)\frac{\partial \Pi_t}{\partial K_t},$$

the derivative with respect to K_{t-1}

$$\frac{\partial V_t(K_{t-1})}{\partial K_{t-1}} = (1-\delta)\frac{\partial \Pi_t}{\partial K_t} + (1-\delta)E\left[\beta_{t+1}\frac{\partial V_{t+1}}{\partial K_t} \mid \Omega_t\right] = 0$$

can be written more informatively

$$\frac{\partial V_t(K_{t-1})}{\partial K_{t-1}} = (1-\delta)\frac{\partial \Pi_t}{\partial K_t} + -(1-\delta)\frac{\partial \Pi_t}{\partial I_t} - (1-\delta)\frac{\partial \Pi_t}{\partial K_t} = 0$$

$$\frac{\partial V_t(K_{t-1})}{\partial K_{t-1}} = -(1-\delta)\frac{\partial \Pi_t}{\partial I_t}$$

The left hand side of the equation is the increase in the value of the firm if it acquires one additional unit of capital in period t-1, which is the shadow value of $(1-\delta)$ units of capital in period t. In other words, the optimality condition is met, if the marginal benefit of investment equals marginal cost of investment.

Because of the assumed convexity of the adjustment costs in investment and decreasing marginal returns of capital, there is an optimal amount of investment. If the shadow value of an additional unit of capital $\frac{\partial V_t(K_{t-1})}{\partial K_{t-1}}$ exceeds the replacement cost of an additional unit of capital $-(1-\delta)\frac{\partial \Pi_t}{\partial I_t}$ an increase in investment will tend to equate the shadow value and the replacement cost. If the shadow value is below replacement cost the amount of investment has to be lower than depreciation or even disinvestments has to take place.[3]

Given the accumulation constraint

$$K_t = (1-\delta)K_{t-1} + I_t$$

and taking the derivative

$$\frac{\partial K_t}{\partial K_{t-1}} = (1-\delta)$$

we find through inserting the derivative of the accumulation constraint the following familiar optimality condition:

$$\frac{\frac{\partial V_t(K_{t-1})}{\partial K_t}}{-\frac{\partial \Pi_t}{\partial I_t}} = 1$$

This optimality condition is rather intuitive. If the optimality condition is fulfilled, the nominator, which contains the change in the value of discounted future profits, equals the denominator, which contains the costs of investment.

3 In this case it has to be assumed that a second hand market to sell capital goods is existent.

2.1.1. The derivation of a linear investment equation

Assuming the markets are competitive, the firm is a price taker in all markets,[4] the change in profits when investing one additional unit is given by

$$\frac{\partial \Pi_t}{\partial I_t} = \frac{\partial\left(p_t\left[F(K_t, L_t) - G(I_t, K_t)\right] - w_t L_t - p_t^I I_t\right)}{\partial I_t}$$

$$\frac{\partial \Pi_t}{\partial I_t} = -p_t \frac{\partial G}{\partial I_t} - p_t^I$$

Using the ratio of the shadow value to the replacement cost

$$\lambda_t = \frac{\partial V_t(K_{t-1})}{\partial K_{t-1}} \frac{1}{(1-\delta)} = -\frac{\partial \Pi_t}{\partial I_t}$$

we obtain

$$\lambda_t = p_t \frac{\partial G}{\partial I_t} + p_t^I$$

$$\frac{\partial G}{\partial I_t} = \frac{\lambda_t - p_t^I}{p_t} = \left(\frac{\lambda_t}{p_t^I} - 1\right)\frac{p_t^I}{p_t}$$

The ratio of the shadow value of capital in period t the price of a unit of investment is known as marginal Q

$$Q = \frac{\lambda_t}{p_t^I}$$

To derive a linear relation between marginal Q and investment some special assumptions about the adjustment cost function have to be made. The following quadratic adjustment cost function is assumed for mathematical convenience (Summers 1981):

---

4 See Worthington (1992) discussing the case of market power.

$$G(I_t,K_t)=\frac{b}{2}\left(\frac{I_t}{K_t}-d\right)^2 K_t .$$

If we take the derivatives of the adjustment function it can be seen that marginal adjustment costs increase linear with the rate of investment

$$\frac{\partial G(I_t,K_t)}{\partial I_t}=b\left(\frac{I_t}{K_t}-d\right)\frac{1}{K_t}K_t=-bd+b\frac{I_t}{K_t}.$$

Using the expression for marginal adjustment cost with marginal Q we have

$$\frac{\partial G}{\partial I_t}=\left(\frac{\lambda_t}{p_t^I}-1\right)\frac{p_t^I}{p_t}=(Q_t-1)\frac{p_t^I}{p_t}=-bd+b\frac{I_t}{K_t}$$

and solving for the investment ratio results in:

$$\frac{I_t}{K_t}=\frac{(Q_t-1)\frac{p_t^I}{p_t}+bd}{b}=d-\frac{1}{b}\frac{p_t^I}{p_t}+\frac{1}{b}\frac{p_t^I}{p_t}Q_t=d+\frac{1}{b}(Q_t-1)\frac{p_t^I}{p_t}$$

Therefore the rate of investment is a linear function of marginal Q.[5]

So far marginal Q has been analyzed. Hayashi (1982) proofed that it is also possible to derive a linear relation between average Q and investment. To derive a simple relation between marginal Q and average Q it is necessary to assume that the production function $F(K_t,L_t)$ and the adjustment cost function $G(I_t,K_t)$ are homogenous of degree one in their arguments. In other words, it is assumed that the production function has constant returns to scale.

Despite this rather restrictive conditions to substitute average Q for marginal Q, in empirical research the use of average Q dominates. Since for the researcher no investment plans concerning one individual investment project are known, the data available usually refer to the firm as a unit. Hence, instead of comparing the induced costs and profits by one single investment project to measure marginal Q, the available

5 When calculating a beginning of period Q empirically we base the calculation on data known to the investor, hence use lagged values only and assume the expectation of the price ratio to equal 1.

discounted sum of future profits, assumed to be mirrored in the stock price, is contrasted with some estimated replacement value to find a measure of average Q. Hence, the availability of public information has to be seen as the main reason why in empirical analysis average Q dominates, rather than theoretical arguments favouring averge Q.

2.2. Investment, information and incentive problems in capital markets

The links between internal funds and investment is interesting from macro- as well as from microeconomic points of view.

From the macroeconomic perspective the relevant question is whether cyclical movements of the economy might be accelerated through the working of „financial factors“.[6] Some authors have labeled the magnification of small initial real shocks by financial market imperfections the „financial accelerator“.[7]

The microeconomic concern lies in the wedge between internal and external costs of finance that might occur because of asymmetric information. When external finance is more costly because of information costs, the neoclassical models based on complete market assumptions leave out important determinants of firms fixed business investment. In that case beside expected future profitability of capital the availability of internal funds plays a crucial role. The lemon premium is a prominent example to show that imperfect information about the quality or riskiness of goods can lead to severe market frictions (Akerlof 1970). In the case of financing risky investment projects the asymmetric information could lead to a gap between the costs of internal funds and the costs of external financing. A second issue is the question how important monitoring costs arising from asymmetric information and incentive problems are on the one hand and how firm's external costs of finance will be affected by the nature of monitoring costs on the other hand.[8] Some models predict cost advantages for firms in a state of constant monitoring through financial intermediaries compared to firms less monitored.[9]

---

6 See the overview article by Taylor (1995).

7 See Bernanke/Gertler/Gilchrist (1996) and Bernanke/Gertler (1990, 1995).

8 See e.g. Diamond (1991).

9 See von Thadden (1990) and Cable (1995).

2.2.1. Illustrating the link between net worth and capital

Fig. 2.1 illustrates the link between internal funds and the firm's optimal choice of the capital stock.[10] The diagram shows the firm's demand for capital ($D(r_i)$) and the supply of funds ($S(W)$) to the firm. The horizontal riskless interest rate r is below the firm's individual interest rate r_i taking into account a constant risk-premium. Because of the downward sloping demand curve, an increase in the interest rate lowers the firms demand for capital. In the case of informational differences between outside investors and firm decision makers, the supply curve might be upward sloping because of lenders asking higher interest rates to cover information costs. Beyond the point of firm's net worth (W) uncollateralized lending will be available at increasing costs only.[11]

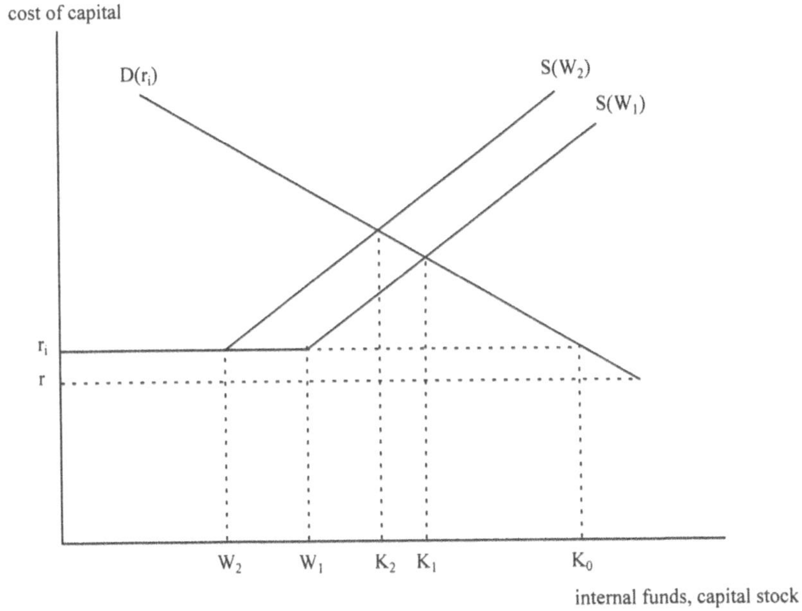

10 See Hubbard (1998) for a similar exposition.

11 See Lamont (1997) for a discussion of internal capital markets. See also Oliner/Rudebusch (1992).

If a firm is operating on it's upward sloping part of the supply curve, the cost of financing investment is a decreasing function of it's internal funds.[12] Given that state of financial constraintness the optimal capital stock for the firm (K_1) is lower than the optimal capital stock under perfect capital market (K_0).

The graph also illustrates the perhaps existing mechanism of accelerating shocks through worsening the financial situation of the firm. Assume a negative shock shifts the demand for investment to the left (to the locus shown in the figure). Simultaneously the internal funds of the firm might be reduced from W_1 to W_2 because of decreasing business activity. The shift of the supply curve to the left exaggerates the negative effect on capital demand through the lowering of internal funds leading to increasing costs of finance ($S(W_2)$). The worsening of the credit conditions lowers the optimal capital stock for the firm from K_1 to K_2.

The aim of the empirical analysis is to address several questions arising from this graphical analysis. Does such an upward sloping part of the capital supply curve caused by information costs exist? How strong is the effect of changes in net worth on investment through an increase in the cost of finance? Are all firms subject to this financial accelerator effect or will only some firms be affected? Is there a classification criterion, which allows distinguishing between classes of firms subject to liquidity constraints and firms that are not?

2.2.2. Empirical tests of Capital-Market Imperfections

The work of John Meyer and Edward Kuh (1957) considered financing constraints as one of the important reasons determining the investment decision. But after the work of Franco Modigliani and Merton Miller (1958) the neoclassical dichotomy again was the theoretical basis and attention focused on real factors solely. The basic finding of Modigliani and Miller was the irrelevance of financial considerations like liquidity, leverage and dividend payments. The user cost model by Jorgenson (1963) and the early works of the *Q*-theory by Tobin (1969) and Hayashi (1982) were formulations of the neoclassical model considering no financial factors.

Gertler describes the dichotomy in an overview article as follows:

---

12 See the discussion in Minton/Schrand (1999).

"Most of macroeconomic theory presumes that the financial systems functions smoothly – and smoothly enough to justify abstracting from financial considerations".[13]

In the last decade empirical research using firm level panel data moved beyond the assumption of the representative firm by modeling firm heterogeneity. The structure of firm level panel data allows differentiating between firms subject to different degrees of financial constraints and facing different information costs. Therefore the availability of firm level panel data gives the opportunity to examine the implications of the theoretical models of asymmetric information on investment.

The major challenge for empirical research is to measure firm's investment opportunities adequately. Because movements in investment opportunities may be linked to movements of internal funds, the finding of correlation between changes in internal net wealth and investment can be caused by underlying movements of investment opportunities only.[14] Using the diagram, there is the need to discriminate between movements of the demand curve, indicating changes in investment opportunities, and movements of the supply curve caused by changes in internal funds.

Because changes in net wealth should stronger effect firms considered as financial constrained, if for example these firms face high information costs, there is the need to find indicators for the level of information costs.

The locus of the supply curve is dependent on the amount of internal funds in the case of information costs; hence there is the need to find proxies for internal funds. The measurement of changes in internal funds should theoretically be uncorrelated with movements in investment opportunities.[15] While it is rather hopeless to find such a proxy it could be hoped for, that controlling for investment opportunities in a multiple regression leaves the proxy of changes in net wealth almost uncorrelated with investment opportunities.

---

13 Gertler (1988), p. 559.

14 See Lang/Stulz/Walking (1991).

15 See Chirinko/Schaller (1995).

2.3. Conclusion

The theoretical framework of the Q-theory of investment is theoretically convincing. Starting with the dynamic optimization problem the firm faces, the investment is shown to be determined by a single measure, Q, containing all information relevant for the firm. The forward-looking character of Q as convincing it is in theory, causes severe problems when turning to an empirical application of the theory. To overcome the fundamental problem of unknown future profits, each attempt to apply the Q-theory has to rely on implicit or explicit forecasts. Hence, while solving the question of the determination of investment behavior theoretically, the Q-theory practically is mainly a shift towards the question of adequate forecasting future profits. Different ways followed in empirical investment research will be discussed in chapter 4.

From the discussion so far it is evident that the correlation found in regressions between cash flow and investment, if cash flow is used as a proxy for changes in net wealth, is hard to interpret. If cash flow correlates with changes in investment opportunities, it is well in accordance with the frictionless neoclassical model that investment correlates with cash flow. Therefore the significance of cash flow parameters in a regression is not a clear sign for the existence of capital-market frictions. These reservations are in place in time series as well as in cross section contexts, because the movements of cash flow can be correlated with movements in investment opportunities over time as well as across firms. Firms facing higher increases in net wealth may face better investment opportunities.

The theoretical correct measure of investment opportunities is the firm's decision maker's expectation of discounted future profits from an additional unit of capital investment. This value is the shadow value of capital to the firm and meets the definition of marginal Q in the neoclassical investment model. Therefore theoretically Q can be seen as a sufficient statistic summarizing all relevant information for the firm's investment decision. Hence, when marginal Q would be taken into account there should be no influence of changes in net wealth (e.g. measured through cash flow) on investment. Unfortunately marginal *Q* is not observable and there is a large literature on how to proxy this key variable as good as possible.[16]

From this context it is obvious, that the less accurate the variable used in regression analysis proxies marginal *Q*, the less clear is the interpretation of the regression results. The more the proxy used deviates from the correct marginal *Q*, the more space is left for cash flow to be significant for measuring investment opportunities beyond measuring pure changes in net wealth.

---

16 See e.g. Klock, Mark / Thies, Clifford F. / Baum, Christohper F. (1991), Whited (1992), Lewellen/Badrinath (1997) and Erickson/Whited (2000b)

3. Dynamic panel data estimation

In this chapter we discusses methods of dynamic panel data estimation. It is well known that the use of the lagged dependent variable as a right hand side variable introduces specific estimation problems, especially the fixed effects estimator becoming biased.

In our analysis we compare several unbiased or near unbiased estimators suggested in the literature. By a Monte Carlo study we assess the bias and efficiency of various proposed estimators under different data generating processes. Especially two classes of estimators will be compared, the class of instrumental estimators, e.g. the well-known Generalized Methods of Moments (GMM) estimator (Arellano/Bond 1991), and the class of direct bias correcting estimators, e.g. the estimator suggested by Kiviet (1995). While in some simulation studies (Kiviet (1995), Judson and Owen (1999), Hansen (2001)) a corrected LSDV estimator is found superior compared to GMM-estimators these simulations take no account of System-GMM-estimators proposed by Blundell and Bond (1998).

After the Monte Carlo study we apply all discussed estimators to estimate a dynamic *Q*-investment function. This application is of interest in several respects. The *Q*-theory can be seen as the standard approach of empirical investment research and the explanation of firm's investment behavior is one of the central issues in empirical economics. Because there exists now a variety of suggested dynamic panel data estimators, it is of interest to assess the differences of the results due to the chosen procedure.

Following the introduction a brief presentation of the problems caused by lagged dependent variables included as right hand side variables in regression functions and the basic idea of GMM is given. In section 3 we discuss several dynamic panel data estimators suggested in the literature. The Monte Carlo simulation is contained in section 4. In section 5 we apply the discussed dynamic panel data estimators to estimate *Q*-investment functions for German manufacturing firms and section 6 concludes.

3.1. The problem of bias caused by lagged dependant variables

The following section explains in short the problem of correlation between explanatory variables and the error term leading to biased estimators.

3.1.1. The idea of instrumentation

The method of instrumentation is one possible way to prevent the bias resulting from correlation between the regressor x and the error term ε. The idea of instrumentation can be stated as follows:

"Find a variable Z, that is highly correlated with X, but does not correlate with ε. Use as the new regressor only that part of the observable variable X which correlates with Z and is orthogonal to ε."

Starting with the problem of correlation between the observable and the error term

$$p\lim\left(\frac{1}{n}X'\varepsilon\right) \neq 0$$

in the linear regression case

$$y = X\beta + \varepsilon \text{ with } \operatorname{var}(\varepsilon) = \sigma^2 I$$

the bias can be circumvented using an instrument Z that correlates with X but is orthogonal to ε:

$$p\lim\left(\frac{1}{n}Z'X\right) = \Sigma_{ZX} \neq 0$$

$$p\lim\left(\frac{1}{n}Z'\varepsilon\right) = 0$$

Premultiplying the regression with Z leads to the residual $Z'\varepsilon$ and the following variance:

$$Z'y = Z'X\beta + Z'\varepsilon$$

$$\operatorname{var}(Z'\varepsilon) = Z' \operatorname{var}(\varepsilon) Z = \sigma^2 Z'Z$$

Making use of the Generalized Least Square-Estimator (GLS) with $V^{-1} = (Z'Z)^{-1}$ and dropping σ^2 leads to the following instrumental variable estimator:

$$b_{IV} = \left[(Z'X)'V^{-1}Z'X\right]^{-1}(Z'X)'V^{-1}Z'y = \left(X'Z(Z'Z)^{-1}Z'X\right)^{-1}X'Z(Z'Z)^{-1}Z'y$$

$$b_{IV} = (X'PX)^{-1} X'Py \qquad \text{with } P = Z(Z'Z)^{-1}Z'$$

Inserting $y = X\beta + \varepsilon$ results in

$$b_{IV} = (X'PX)^{-1} X'P(X\beta + \varepsilon) = (X'PX)^{-1} X'PX\beta + (X'PX)^{-1} X'P\varepsilon$$

$$= \left(X'Z(Z'Z)^{-1}Z'X\right)^{-1} X'Z(Z'Z)^{-1}Z'X\beta + \left(X'Z(Z'Z)^{-1}Z'X\right)^{-1} X'Z(Z'Z)^{-1}Z'\varepsilon$$

$$= \beta + \left(\frac{1}{n}X'Z(Z'Z)^{-1}Z'X\right)^{-1} \frac{1}{n}X'Z(Z'Z)^{-1}Z'\varepsilon$$

Now taking probability limits shows the estimator being unbiased:

$$p\lim b_{IV} = \beta + P\lim\left[\left(\frac{1}{n}X'Z(Z'Z)^{-1}Z'X\right)^{-1} \frac{1}{n}X'Z(Z'Z)^{-1}Z'\varepsilon\right]$$

$$p\lim b_{IV} = \beta + \left(\Sigma_{XZ}\Sigma_{ZZ}^{-1}\Sigma_{ZX}\right)^{-1} \Sigma_{XZ}\Sigma_{ZZ}^{-1}\Sigma_{Z\varepsilon} = \beta$$

where we make use of $\Sigma_{Z\varepsilon} = 0$.

Therefore it is evident, that basic to the idea of instrumenting is the assumed uncorrelatedness of Z and ε.

The instrumentation can be made transparent through the exposition as a two-stage procedure. In the first step the explanatory variable X is regressed on the instrument Z. The regression values $\hat{X}$ containing the linear dependent part of X are used as explanatory variables in the second step.

Based on the first auxiliary regression

$$X = Z\gamma + v,$$

regression values are obtained

$$\hat{X} = Z\hat{\gamma} = Z(Z'Z)^{-1}Z'X,$$

which will be used as new regressors in the second stage

$$y = \hat{X} b_{2S} + \varepsilon$$

$$b_{2S} = \left(\hat{X}'\hat{X}\right)^{-1} \hat{X}'y .$$

Inserting $Z(Z'Z)^{-1}Z'X$ for the regression values $\hat{X}$ leads to the instrumental variable estimator b_{IV}:

$$b_{2S} = \left(\left(Z(Z'Z)^{-1}Z'X\right)' Z(Z'Z)^{-1}Z'X\right)^{-1} \left(Z(Z'Z)^{-1}Z'X\right)' y$$

$$= \left(X'Z(ZZ')^{-1}Z'Z(Z'Z)^{-1}Z'X\right)^{-1} X'Z(ZZ')^{-1}Z'y$$

$$\left(X'Z(ZZ')^{-1}Z'X\right)^{-1} X'Z(ZZ')^{-1}Z'y = (X'PX)^{-1}X'Py = b_{IV}$$

3.1.2. Generalized Methods of Moments (GMM)

During the last decade the concept of Generalized Methods of Moments (GMM) has become increasingly popular. Before discussing some dynamic panel data estimators based on the ideas of GMM, the basic concept is introduced.[1]

The concept of GMM is often a simple alternative, if the explicit Maximum-Likelihood function is difficult to derive. The core of the GMM-estimation is the use of orthogonality conditions. In general GMM can be seen as being especially suited for large data files, while when using only few observations GMM is often less efficient then alternative methods.

The simple OLS-estimation can be represented as an application of the method of moments. The condition of uncorrelatedness of the explanatory variable and the error term is the point to start from:

$$E(X'\varepsilon) = 0$$

---

1 See e.g. the introduction by Mátyás/Harris (1999).

Applying this condition to the sample results in the following conditions:

$$\frac{1}{n}X'\left(y - X\hat{\beta}\right) = 0$$

Solving this equation for the parameter vector results in the well know OLS-estimator:

$$\hat{\beta} = (X'X)^{-1}X'y$$

In the same fashion the instrumentation can be expressed as an application of the method of moments where use is made of the assumption that the instrument is orthogonal to the error term:

$$E(Z'\varepsilon) = 0$$

Applying this condition to the sample

$$\frac{1}{n}Z'\left(y - X\hat{\beta}\right) = 0$$

and solving for the parameter vector results in

$$\hat{\beta}_{IV} = b_{2S} = (X'PX)^{-1}X'Py$$

$$\text{with } P = Z(Z'Z)^{-1}Z'$$

when applying GLS with $V^{-1} = (Z'Z)^{-1}$. If the number of instruments equals the number of explanatory variables, the estimator simplifies to

$$\hat{\beta}_{IV} = (Z'X)^{-1}Z'y.$$

3.2. Dynamic panel data estimators

In this section we discuss several suggested estimators for dynamic panel data models. The starting point is the well-known bias of the fixed effects model (Nickell 1981), which would be the natural choice when allowing for individual effects.[2]

3.2.1. The bias of the fixed effects model

The linear model to estimate contains explanatory variables x_t as well as the lagged endogenous variable y_{t-1}.

$$y_{it} = \rho y_{i,t-1} + x'_{it}\beta + \alpha_i + \varepsilon_{it}$$

$$\text{where} \quad \varepsilon_{it} \sim N\left(0, \sigma_\varepsilon^2\right) \qquad \text{and} \qquad |\rho| < 1$$

$i = 1,...,N$ index for individuals

$t = 1,...,T$ index for years

x'_{it} row vector of explanatory variables, dimension k

ρ unknown parameter of the lagged endogenous variable

β unknown parameter vector of the k explanatory variables

α_i individual specific fixed effects

Further we make the following assumptions:

- the error term is orthogonal to the exogenous variables: $E\left(x'_{it}\varepsilon_{it}\right) = 0$

- the exogenous variables might be correlated with the individual effect $E\left(x'_{it}\alpha_i\right) \neq 0$

- the error term (i.i.d.) is uncorrelated with the lagged endogenous variable: $E\left(y_{i,t-1}\varepsilon_{it}\right) = 0$

Using matrix notation the model can be expressed as

2 For an overview of dynamic panel data estimation see Mátyás/Sevestre (1995) and Baltagi (2001).

$$y = y_{-1}\rho + X\beta + D\alpha + \varepsilon$$

where

$$y = \begin{pmatrix} y_1 \\ y_2 \\ \vdots \\ y_N \end{pmatrix} \quad y_i = \begin{pmatrix} y_{i1} \\ y_{i2} \\ \vdots \\ y_{iT} \end{pmatrix} \quad X = \begin{pmatrix} X_1 \\ X_2 \\ \vdots \\ X_N \end{pmatrix} \quad X_i = \begin{pmatrix} x'_{i1} \\ x'_{i2} \\ \vdots \\ x'_{iT} \end{pmatrix}$$

$$D = I_N \otimes e \quad e = \begin{pmatrix} 1 \\ 1 \\ \vdots \\ 1 \end{pmatrix} \text{with dimension } T \quad \alpha = \begin{pmatrix} \alpha_1 \\ \alpha_2 \\ \vdots \\ \alpha_N \end{pmatrix}$$

The simple Least Squares Dummy Variable Estimator (LSDV) is

$$My = My_{-1}\rho + MX\beta + M\varepsilon$$

$$y^* = y^*_{-1}\,\rho + X^*\beta + \varepsilon^*$$

where

$$M = I_{NT} - D(D'D)^{-1}D' = I_N \otimes I_T - I_N \otimes \frac{1}{T}ee' = I_N \otimes \left(I_T - \frac{1}{T}ee' \right).$$

Premultiplying with matrix M results in variables measured as deviations from the individual specific means. Because the demeaning procedure makes use of all available time periods,

$$y^*_{i,t-1} = y_{i,t-1} - \frac{1}{T}\sum_{t=1}^{T} y_{i,t-1}$$

$$\varepsilon^*_{it} = \varepsilon_{it} - \frac{1}{T}\sum_{t=1}^{T} \varepsilon_{it}$$

the demeaned lagged endogenous variable correlates with the demeaned error term:

$$E\left(y^*_{i,t-1}\,\varepsilon^*_{it}\right) \neq 0.$$

The error term $\varepsilon_{i,t-1}$ is contained with the weight $1-\frac{1}{T}$ in $y^*_{i,t-1}$ and with the weight $-\frac{1}{T}$ in $\varepsilon^*_{i,t}$. This correlation renders the LSDV-estimators $\hat{\rho}$ and $\hat{\beta}$ biased. It is also obvious that the correlation decreases in *T*, the number of years available. But since a typical microeconomic panel contains a large number of individuals *N* but only a few periods of time *T*, the asymptotic behavior of the estimator is of special interest when *N* tends to infinity ($N \to \infty$). The asymptotic bias of the LSDV-estimator was derived by Nickell (1981):

$$\operatorname*{plim}_{N\to\infty}(\hat{\rho}-\rho)=\left(\operatorname*{plim}_{N\to\infty}\frac{1}{NT}y^{*\prime}_{-1}\,Py^*_{-1}\right)^{-1}\frac{-\sigma_\varepsilon^2}{T(1-\rho)}\left(1-\frac{1}{T}\frac{\left(1-\rho^T\right)}{T(1-\rho)}\right)$$

where $P = I_{NT} - X^*(X^{*\prime}X^*)^{-1}X^*$ is the residual maker.

Inserting *P* into the bias expressions leads to

$$\operatorname*{plim}_{N\to\infty}(\hat{\rho}-\rho)=\left(\operatorname*{plim}_{N\to\infty}\frac{1}{NT}y^{*\prime}_{-1}\left(I_{NT}-X^*(X^{*\prime}X^*)^{-1}X^{*\prime}\right)y^*_{-1}\right)^{-1}\frac{-\sigma_\varepsilon^2}{T(1-\rho)}\left(1-\frac{1}{T}\frac{\left(1-\rho^T\right)}{T(1-\rho)}\right)$$

$$=\left(\operatorname*{plim}_{N\to\infty}\frac{1}{NT}y^{*\prime}_{-1}\left(y^*_{-1}-X^*\hat{\beta}\right)\right)^{-1}\frac{-\sigma_\varepsilon^2}{T(1-\rho)}\left(1-\frac{1}{T}\frac{\left(1-\rho^T\right)}{T(1-\rho)}\right)$$

$$=\left(\operatorname*{plim}_{N\to\infty}\frac{1}{NT}y^{*\prime}_{-1}\,\varepsilon^*_{-1}\right)^{-1}\frac{-\sigma_\varepsilon^2}{T(1-\rho)}\left(1-\frac{1}{T}\frac{\left(1-\rho^T\right)}{T(1-\rho)}\right)$$

The asymptotic bias of the parameter vector $\hat{\beta}$ of the remaining explanatory variables is given by:

$$\operatorname*{plim}_{N\to\infty}\left(\hat{\beta}-\beta\right)=-\operatorname*{plim}_{N\to\infty}\left((X^{*\prime}X^*)^{-1}X^{*\prime}y^*_{-1}\right)\operatorname*{plim}_{N\to\infty}(\hat{\rho}-\rho)$$

$$=-\operatorname*{plim}_{N\to\infty}\hat{\beta}\operatorname*{plim}_{N\to\infty}(\hat{\rho}-\rho).$$

The asymptotic bias $\hat{\rho}-\rho$ is growing in ρ, N, σ_ε^2 and in the sum of squares $\varepsilon^*{}_{-1}{}' \varepsilon^*{}_{-1}$, while it is decreasing in T.

3.2.2. Some proposed dynamic panel data estimators

In the following we discuss some dynamic panel data estimators proposed in the literature, which will be examined in a Monte Carlo study. In the following we assume the explanatory variables to be at least predetermined what leads to the assumption of

$$E(x_{it}\varepsilon_{is})=0 \text{ for } s \geq t \text{ but } E(x_{it}\varepsilon_{is}) \neq 0 \text{ for } s<t.$$

3.2.2.1. The Anderson-Hsiao estimator

The estimator suggested by Anderson and Hsiao (1982) is based on the differenced form of the original equation[3]

$$y_{it} = \rho y_{i,t-1} + x_{it}'\beta + \alpha_i + \varepsilon_{it}$$

$$y_{it} - y_{i,t-1} = \rho(y_{i,t-1} - y_{i,t-2}) + (x_{it}' - x_{i,t-1}')\beta + \varepsilon_{it} - \varepsilon_{i,t-1}$$

which cancels the individual fixed effects assumed to possibly correlate with the exogenous variables $(E(x_{it}'\alpha_i) \neq 0)$. Using matrix notation we can write

$$y = y_{-1}\rho + X\beta + D\alpha + \varepsilon$$

$$Fy = Fy_{-1}\rho + FX\beta + F\varepsilon$$

where

$$F = I_N \otimes F_T \text{ and } F_T = \begin{pmatrix} -1 & 1 & 0 & \cdots & 0 & 0 \\ 0 & -1 & 1 & \cdots & 0 & 0 \\ \vdots & & & & & \\ 0 & 0 & 0 & \cdots & -1 & 1 \end{pmatrix} \text{ with dimension } (T-1)\times T.$$

Because $FD=0$, the individual fixed effects cancel out. But the difference of the lagged endogenous variable

---

3 See also Anderson/Hsiao (1981).

$$y_{i,t-1} - y_{i,t-2} = \rho\left(y_{i,t-2} - y_{i,t-3}\right) + \left(x'_{i,t-1} - x'_{i,t-2}\right)\beta + \varepsilon_{i,t-1} - \varepsilon_{i,t-2}$$

is now obviously correlated with the error term

$$\varepsilon_{it} - \varepsilon_{i,t-1}.$$

Therefore $E\left(dy_{i,t-1} d\varepsilon_{it}\right) \neq 0$ and the estimator will be biased.

Anderson and Hsiao suggest using level instruments y_{t-2} or the lagged difference $y_{i,t-2} - y_{i,t-3}$ as an instrument for the differenced lagged endogenous regressor $y_{i,t-1} - y_{i,t-2}$. These instruments can be expected to be uncorrelated with the differenced error term:

$$E\left(y_{i,t-2} d\varepsilon_{it}\right) = 0 \text{ and } E\left(dy_{i,t-2} d\varepsilon_{it}\right) = 0 .$$

When analyzing the properties of the two possible instruments Arellano (1989) found the estimator using level instruments superior because of having smaller variances and no points of singularities. Furthermore the use of the levels as instruments has the advantage of loosing one year less what can be relevant in the practical use, especially when using data files with a large number of individuals and few years.

The differencing imposes a MA(1) structure on the error term, even when the errors ε_{it} originally where not correlated over time.

Estimation will then make use of the following matrices in the case of levels as instruments:

$$\widetilde{Z}_i = \begin{bmatrix} y_{i,1} & x'_{i3} - x'_{i2} \\ y_{i,2} & x'_{i4} - x'_{i3} \\ \vdots & \vdots \\ y_{i,T-2} & x'_{iT} - x'_{i,T-1} \end{bmatrix}$$

$$\widetilde{X}_i = \begin{bmatrix} y_{i2} - y_{i1} & x'_{i3} - x'_{i2} \\ y_{i3} - y_{i,2} & x'_{i4} - x'_{3} \\ \vdots & \vdots \\ y_{i,T-1} - y_{i,T-2} & x'_{iT} - x'_{i,T-1} \end{bmatrix}$$

$$\widetilde{y}_i = \begin{bmatrix} y_{i3} - y_{i,2} \\ y_{i4} - y_{i,3} \\ \vdots \\ y_{i,T} - y_{i,T-1} \end{bmatrix}.$$

And as follows for the use of differenced instruments:

$$\widetilde{X}_i = \begin{bmatrix} y_{i3} - y_{i2} & x'_{i4} - x'_{i3} \\ y_{i4} - y_{i,3} & x'_{i5} - x'_{4} \\ \vdots & \vdots \\ y_{i,T-1} - y_{i,T-2} & x'_{iT} - x'_{i,T-1} \end{bmatrix}$$

$$\widetilde{Z}_i = \begin{bmatrix} y_{i2} - y_{i1} & x'_{i4} - x'_{i3} \\ y_{i3} - y_{i,2} & x'_{i5} - x'_{i4} \\ \vdots & \vdots \\ y_{i,T-2} - y_{i,T-3} & x'_{iT} - x'_{i,T-1} \end{bmatrix}$$

$$\widetilde{y}_i = \begin{bmatrix} y_{i4} - y_{i,3} \\ y_{i5} - y_{i,4} \\ \vdots \\ y_{i,T} - y_{i,T-1} \end{bmatrix}.$$

Stacking the observations for all individuals results in the two estimators:

$$Z = \begin{bmatrix} \widetilde{Z}_1 \\ \widetilde{Z}_2 \\ \vdots \\ \widetilde{Z}_N \end{bmatrix}, \quad X = \begin{bmatrix} \widetilde{X}_1 \\ \widetilde{X}_2 \\ \vdots \\ \widetilde{X}_N \end{bmatrix}, \quad y = \begin{bmatrix} \widetilde{y}_1 \\ \widetilde{y}_2 \\ \vdots \\ \widetilde{y}_N \end{bmatrix}$$

$$\hat{\gamma}^{AH} = (XPX)^{-1} X'Py \quad \text{where} \quad P = Z(Z'Z)^{-1} Z'.$$

We add the symbol L or D to indicate the use of levels or differences as instruments ($\hat{\gamma}^{AH,L}, \hat{\gamma}^{AH,D}$).

3.2.2.2. The Arellano-Bond estimator

In empirical work using firm level or household panel data the Generalized Method of Moments estimator (GMM) suggested by Arrelano and Bond (1991) has become increasingly popular. The estimator is similar to the estimator suggested by Anderson and Hsiao but exploits additional moment restrictions, which enlarges the set of instruments.

The dynamic equation to be estimated in levels is

$$y_{it} = \rho y_{i,t-1} + x'_{it}\beta + \alpha_i + \varepsilon_{it}$$

where differencing eliminates the individual effects α_i:

$$y_{it} - y_{i,t-1} = \rho(y_{i,t-1} - y_{i,t-2}) + (x'_{it} - x'_{i,t-1})\beta + \varepsilon_{it} - \varepsilon_{i,t-1}$$

For each year we now look for the instruments available for instrumenting the difference equation. For $t = 3$ the equation to be estimated is

$$y_{i3} - y_{i2} = \rho(y_{i2} - y_{i1}) + (x'_{i3} - x'_{i2})\beta + \varepsilon_{i3} - \varepsilon_{i2}$$

where the instruments (again assuming x being at least predetermined) $y_{i,1}$, x'_{i2} and x'_{i1} are available.

For $t = 4$ the equation is

$$y_{i4} - y_{i3} = \rho(y_{i3} - y_{i2}) + (x'_{i4} - x'_{i3})\beta + \varepsilon_{i4} - \varepsilon_{i3}$$

and the instruments $y_{i,1}, y_{i,2}, x'_{i1}, x'_{i2}$ and x'_{i3} are available. As can be seen, the time periods valid for instrumentation enlarge and for the equation in the final Period T

$$y_{iT} - y_{i,T-1} = \rho(y_{i,T-1} - y_{i,T-2}) + (x'_{iT} - x'_{i,T-1})\beta + \varepsilon_{iT} - \varepsilon_{i,T-1}$$

the instruments $y_{i,1}, y_{i,2}, \ldots, y_{i,T-2}, x'_{i1}, x'_{i2}, \ldots, x'_{i,T-1}$ are available.

The instrumented equation is

$$W'Fy = W'FX\gamma + W'F\varepsilon$$

where

$$X_i = \begin{bmatrix} y_{i2} - y_{i1} & x'_{i3} - x'_{i2} \\ y_{i3} - y_{i,2} & x'_{i4} - x'_{i3} \\ \vdots & \vdots \\ y_{i,T-1} - y_{i,T-2} & x'_{iT} - x'_{i,T-1} \end{bmatrix}$$

$$X = (y_{-1}, X), \quad \gamma' = (\rho, \beta'), \quad W = \left(W_1', W_2', \ldots, W_N'\right)'$$

$$W_i = \begin{bmatrix} [y_{i1}, x'_{i1}, x'_{i2}] & 0 & \cdots & 0 \\ 0 & [y_{i1}, y_{i2}, x'_{i1}, x'_{i2}, x'_{i3}] & \cdots & 0 \\ 0 & 0 & \ddots & 0 \\ \vdots & \vdots & & \vdots \\ 0 & 0 & \cdots & [y_{i1}, y_{i2}, \ldots y_{i,T-2}, x'_{i1}, x'_{i2}, \ldots, x'_{iT-1}] \end{bmatrix}$$

As has been shown for the simple case of the instrumental variable estimation, the estimation procedure can be seen as a two-step estimation. First a cross-section auxiliary equation

$$y_{i,t} - y_{i,t-1} = \hat{a}_{1t} y_{i,t-2} + \hat{a}_{2t} y_{i,t-3} + \ldots + x'_{it-1} \hat{b}_{1t} + x'_{it-2} \hat{b}_{2t} + \ldots + v_{it}$$

is estimated and in the second step the resulting estimates are used as explanatory variables in the equation of original interest.

In the *k*-explanatory variable case the maximal number of parameters to be estimated is $T - 2 + k(T-1) = (k+1)(T-1) - 1$, which determines the number of individuals necessary to allow estimation.

Because the differencing operation introduces first order autocorrelation into the error term, the first-step estimator makes use of a covariance matrix taking this autocorrelation into account.

$$V = W'GW = \sum_{i=1}^{N} W_i' G_T W_i$$

where $G = \left(I_N \otimes G_T'\right)$ and $G_T = F_T F_T' = \begin{bmatrix} 2 & -1 & & 0 \\ -1 & 2 & \ddots & \\ & \ddots & \ddots & -1 \\ 0 & & -1 & 2 \end{bmatrix}$.

Premultiplying the matrix F results in transforming the original observations into differences. Because $Var(Fu) = F\sigma^2 F'$, the covariance matrix $V = FF'$ is used as a first-step approximation to the covariance matrix.

The two-step GMM estimator uses the residuals of the first-step estimation to estimate the covariance matrix as suggested by White (1980):

$$\hat{V} = \sum_{i=1}^{N} W_i' F_T \hat{\varepsilon}_i \hat{\varepsilon}_i' F_T' W_i$$

The resulting estimator finally is

$$\hat{\gamma}^{GMM} = \left(X'W\hat{V}^{-1}W'X\right)^{-1} X'W\hat{V}^{-1}W'y.$$

3.2.2.3. The Blundell-Bond estimator

The GMM estimator, which was suggested by Arellano and Bond (1991), is known to be rather inefficient when instruments are weak because making use of the information contained in differences only. In their 1998 paper Blundell and Bond suggest making use of additional level information beside the differences. The combination of moment restrictions for differences and levels results in an estimator, which was called GMM-system-estimator by Arrellano and Bond.

There are T-2 othogonality restrictions in levels, which are exploited. The observation t in levels

$$y_{it} = \rho y_{i,t-1} + x_{it}'\beta + \alpha_i + \varepsilon_{it}$$

will be used for the estimation, where differences are used as valid instruments (again assuming x being at least predetermined).

Take for example the last observation T:

$$y_{iT} = \rho y_{i,T-1} + x_{iT}'\beta + \alpha_i + \varepsilon_{iT}$$

where use is made of the instruments $dy_{i,1}, dy_{i,2}, \ldots, dy_{i,T-1}, dx_{i1}', dx_{i2}', \ldots, dx_{i,T}'$.

The matrices used for estimation are then defined as:

$$y_i = \begin{bmatrix} y_{i3} - y_{i,2} \\ y_{i4} - y_{i,3} \\ \vdots \\ y_{i,T} - y_{i,T-1} \\ y_{i3} \\ \vdots \\ y_{iT} \end{bmatrix} \qquad X_i = \begin{bmatrix} y_{i2} - y_{i1} & x'_{i3} - x'_{i2} \\ y_{i3} - y_{i,2} & x'_{i4} - x'_{i3} \\ \vdots & \vdots \\ y_{i,T-1} - y_{i,T-2} & x'_{iT} - x'_{i,T-1} \\ y_{i,2} & x'_{i2} \\ \vdots & \vdots \\ y_{i,T-1} & x'_{iT} \end{bmatrix}$$

$$\tilde{X} = (y_{-1}, X), \quad \gamma' = (\rho, \beta'), \quad W = (W_1{}', W_2{}', \ldots, W_N{}')'$$

$$W_i^D = \begin{bmatrix} [y_{i1}, x'_{i1}, x'_{i2}] & 0 & \cdots & 0 \\ 0 & [y_{i1}, y_{i2}, x'_{i1}, x'_{i2}, x'_{i3}] & \cdots & 0 \\ 0 & 0 & \ddots & 0 \\ \vdots & \vdots & & \vdots \\ 0 & 0 & \cdots & [y_{i1}, y_{i2}, \ldots y_{i,T-2}, x'_{i1}, x'_{i2}, \ldots, x'_{iT-1}] \end{bmatrix}$$

$$W_i^L = \begin{bmatrix} [dy_{i2}, dx'_{i2}, dx'_{i3}] & 0 & \cdots & 0 \\ 0 & [dy'_{i2}, dy'_{i3}, dx'_{i2}, dx'_{i3}, dx'_{i4}] & \cdots & 0 \\ 0 & 0 & \ddots & 0 \\ \vdots & \vdots & & \vdots \\ 0 & 0 & \cdots & [dy'_{i2}, \ldots dy_{i,T-2}, dx'_{i2}, \ldots, dx'_{iT-1} \end{bmatrix}$$

$$W_i = \begin{bmatrix} W_i^D & 0 \\ 0 & W_i^L \end{bmatrix}$$

The first-step estimator makes use of a covariance matrix taking this autocorrelation into account enlarged for the level equations.

$$V = W'GW = \sum_{i=1}^{N} W_i' G_T W_i$$

where $G=\left(I_N \otimes G^{D,L'}\right)$ and $G^D=\begin{bmatrix} 2 & -1 & & 0 \\ -1 & 2 & \ddots & \\ & \ddots & \ddots & -1 \\ 0 & & -1 & 2 \end{bmatrix}$.

$$G^L=\begin{bmatrix} 1 & 0 & & 0 \\ 0 & 1 & \ddots & \\ & \ddots & \ddots & 0 \\ 0 & & 0 & 1 \end{bmatrix}$$

$$G^{D,L}=\begin{bmatrix} W_i^D & 0 \\ 0 & W_i^L \end{bmatrix}$$

The two-step GMM estimator uses the residuals of the first-step estimation to estimate the covariance matrix as suggested by White (1980):

$$\hat{V}=\sum_{i=1}^{N} W_i' F_T \hat{\varepsilon}_i \hat{\varepsilon}_i' F_T' W_i$$

The resulting estimator finally is

$$\hat{\gamma}^{GMM-SYS}=\left(X'W\hat{V}^{-1}W'X\right)^{-1}X'W\hat{V}^{-1}W'y.$$

3.2.2.4. The direct bias correction

Making use of the asymptotic bias expression derived by Nickell, Kiviet (1995) proposed a direct bias correction method. The basic idea is the approximation of the unknown bias by a two-step procedure. While in the first round empirical estimates are derived, in the second step by a plug-in-procedure an empirical estimation of the bias is derived which leads to a correction of the biased fixed effects estimator.

The motivation for the direct correction lies in the well known fact, that the Least-Squares-Dummy-Variable estimator (LSDV) is biased but has a variance much smaller compared to instrumental variables estimators, like the Anderson-Hsiao estimator.

Kiviet derives the following approximation for the expected bias:

$$\hat{\gamma}-\gamma=-\sigma_{\varepsilon}^{2}(D)^{-1}\begin{pmatrix}\frac{N}{T}(j_t'Cj_t)\left(2q-\overline{W}'A\overline{W}(D)^{-1}q\right)\\+tr\left(\overline{W}'(I_N\otimes A_TCA_T)\overline{W}(D)^{-1}\right)q\\+\overline{W}'(I_N\otimes A_TCA_T)\overline{W}(D)^{-1}q+\sigma_{\varepsilon}^{2}Nq'(D)^{-1}q\\\times\left(-\frac{N}{T}(j_t'Cj_t)tr(C'A_TC)+2tr(C'A_TCA_TC)\right)q\end{pmatrix}$$

with

$$D=\overline{W}'A\overline{W}+\sigma_{\varepsilon}^{2}Ntr(C'A_TC)qq'$$

$$A\overline{W}=E(AW)$$

$$W=[y_{-1}\ \vdots\ X]$$

$$\gamma'=[\rho,\beta']$$

$$A_T=I_T-\frac{1}{T}j_Tj_T{}'$$

$$A=I_N\otimes A_T$$

$$C=\begin{bmatrix}0&.&.&.&.&.&0\\1&0&&&&&.\\\lambda&1&0&&&&.\\\lambda^2&&1&.&&&.\\.&.&.&.&.&&.\\.&&&.&.&.&.\\\lambda^{T-2}&.&.&.&\lambda&1&0\end{bmatrix}$$

where λ is a first round estimate of ρ, the parameter of the lagged endogenous variable and

$q=(1,0,...,0)'$ with dimension k+1, where k is the number of exogenous variables.

Kiviet suggests the use of a consistent first round estimator, e.g. the Anderson-Hsiao instrumental variable estimator. In our simulations we will make use of the LSDV-estimator and the first step GMM estimator in the first round respectively.

3.2.2.5. An alternative bias correction method

Based on the estimator proposed by Kiviet (1995) Hansen (2001) suggested an alternative bias correction method. The basic idea is the approximation of the unknown bias by making use of the first step biased fixed effects estimator. As the starting point the biased fixed effects estimators $\hat{\rho}$ and $\hat{\beta}$ are obtained. Making use of first round regression results the asymptotic bias expression is approximated.

The term

$$\left(\underset{N \to \infty}{p\lim} \frac{1}{NT} y^{*\prime}_{-1}\, \varepsilon^*_{-1} \right)^{-1}$$

is approximated by

$$\frac{NT}{\varepsilon^{*\prime}_{-1}\, \varepsilon^*_{-1}}$$

and

$$\frac{-\sigma_\varepsilon^2}{T(1-\rho)}\left(1-\frac{1}{T}\frac{(1-\rho')}{T(1-\rho)}\right)$$

by

$$\frac{-\hat{\sigma}_\varepsilon^2}{T(1-\hat{\rho})}\left(1-\frac{1}{T}\frac{(1-\hat{\rho}')}{T(1-\hat{\rho})}\right)$$

using $\varepsilon^*_{i,t-1} = y^*_{-1} - X^* \hat{\beta}$ and $\hat{\beta} = (X^{*\prime} X^*)^{-1} X^{*\prime} y^*_{-1}$.

Now the parameter $\hat{\rho}_C$ is estimated, which minimizes the quadratic difference between the unknown bias and the approximated bias on the basis of the first step fixed effects estimation.

$$\hat{\rho}_C : \underset{\rho}{Min}\left[Bias - B\hat{i}as\right]^2$$

$$\hat{\rho}_C : \underset{\rho}{Min}\left[(\hat{\rho}-\rho) - \frac{NT}{\varepsilon^{*\prime}_{-1}\, \varepsilon^*_{-1}} \frac{-\hat{\sigma}_\varepsilon^2}{T(1-\rho)}\left(1-\frac{1}{T}\frac{(1-\rho')}{T(1-\rho)}\right)\right]^2$$

The problem has to be solved iteratively. Because the unknown parameter ρ is expected to be in a rather narrow interval, a grid-search is applied.

By making use of the bias corrected parameter of the lagged endogenous variable $\hat{\rho}_c$ the bias corrected estimator for the exogenous variables $\hat{\beta}_c$ is estimated making again use of the first step regression results:

$$\underset{N\to\infty}{p\lim}(\hat{\beta}-\beta) = -\underset{N\to\infty}{p\lim}\left((X^{*\prime}X^{*})^{-1}X^{*\prime}y^{*}_{-1}\right)\underset{N\to\infty}{p\lim}(\hat{\rho}-\rho)$$

$$\hat{\beta}_c = \hat{\beta} + \hat{\beta}(\hat{\rho}-\hat{\rho}_c).$$

3.3. Monte Carlo study

The following Monte Carlo study compares the behavior of the different discussed estimators under different circumstances. We vary the size of the data set as well as various key parameters in the simulation setting. Besides analyzing the bias of the estimators the study enables to assess the reliability of the estimated standard deviations. The Root Mean Square Error (RMSE) criterion is used to assess the efficiency of the estimators.

All simulations were carried out using estimation routines written in the Interactive Matrix Language (IML) contained in the SAS software package by the author. The number of simulation runs is 2,000 throughout this chapter.

3.3.1. The case of a strictly exogenous explanatory variable

The simulation is based on the following model:

$$y_{it} = \rho y_{i,t-1} + x'_{it-1}\beta + \alpha_i + \varepsilon_{it} \qquad \text{where } \varepsilon_{it} \sim N(0,\sigma_\varepsilon^2) \text{ and } \alpha_i \sim N(0,\sigma_\alpha^2)$$

$$x_{it} = \eta\, x_{i,t-1} + \zeta_{it} \qquad \text{where } \zeta_{it} \sim N(0,\sigma_\zeta^2)$$

$$\gamma = (\rho\ \beta)' \qquad \beta = 1 \quad \rho = \{0.1, 0.5, 0.9\} \qquad \eta = \{0.1, 0.5, 0.9\}$$

Because all the estimators, except the simple pooled estimator in levels, allow for a possible correlation of the individual effects a_i and the explanatory variable $\bar{x}_i$, we do not consider such correlation in the simulation. For each individual the first 20 simulated data were dropped.

The following tables contain simulation results. The means of the estimators $(\overline{X})$ as well as the mean of the estimated standard deviations $\overline{\hat{std}}$, the empirical standard deviation (*std*) of the estimators in the simulation runs as well as the RMSE. Table 1 contains the results of the simulation for 100 individuals.

We consider the following estimators:

γ^{Pooled}	Pooled estimator
γ^{LSDV}	Least Squares Dummy Variable Model (LSDV)
$\gamma^{AH,L}$	Anderson-Hsiao estimator using lagged levels as instruments (AH,L)
$\gamma^{AH,D}$	Anderson-Hsiao estimator using lagged differences as instruments
$\gamma^{BC,H}$	Bias corrected estimator using proposed by Hansen (BC,H)
$\gamma^{BC,K1}$	Bias corrected estimator using proposed by Kiviet, using LSDV in first step (BC,K1)
$\gamma^{BC,K2}$	Bias corrected estimator using proposed by Kiviet, using GMM1 in first step (BC,K2)
γ^{GMM1}	First step Arellano-Bond estimator (GMM1)
γ^{GMM2}	Second step Arellano-Bond estimator using estimated covariance matrix (GMM2)
γ^{SYS1}	First step system-estimator using level and differences as instruments proposed by Blundell and Bond (SYS1)
γ^{SYS2}	Second step system-estimator using estimated covariance matrix proposed by Blundell and Bond (SYS2)

Table 3.1: Simulation results, T=10, N=100 , $\sigma_\varepsilon^2 = 1$, $\rho = 0.5$, $\eta = 0.5$

	ρ				β			
	$\overline{X}$	$\overline{s\hat{t}d}$	std	$RMSE$	$\overline{X}$	$\overline{s\hat{t}d}$	std	$RMSE$
γ^{Pooled}	0.708	0.014	0.021	0.209	0.655	0.029	0.043	0.348
γ^{LSDV}	0.429	0.021	0.021	0.074	1.019	0.034	0.033	0.038
$\gamma^{AH,L}$	0.498	0.178	0.083	0.082	1.001	0.073	0.05	0.05
$\gamma^{AH,D}$	0.96	63.08	5.489	5.494	1.101	12.716	1.103	1.105
$\gamma^{BC,H}$	0.497	0.021	0.022	0.022	1.002	0.034	0.032	0.032
$\gamma^{BC,K1}$	0.481	0.021	0.022	0.029	0.959	0.034	0.031	0.051
$\gamma^{BC,K2}$	0.484	0.021	0.022	0.027	0.957	0.034	0.031	0.053
γ^{GMM1}	0.475	0.033	0.033	0.042	0.986	0.059	0.063	0.064
γ^{GMM2}	0.474	0.013	0.036	0.044	0.984	0.024	0.066	0.068
γ^{SYS1}	0.504	0.029	0.031	0.031	1.006	0.05	0.054	0.054
γ^{SYS2}	0.504	0.004	0.031	0.031	1.007	0.007	0.053	0.054

To ease the comparison of the results for the different estimators, the following figure illustrates the bias and the RMSE for the estimators.

Fig. 3.1: Bias and Root Mean Square Error of ρ, N=100[4]

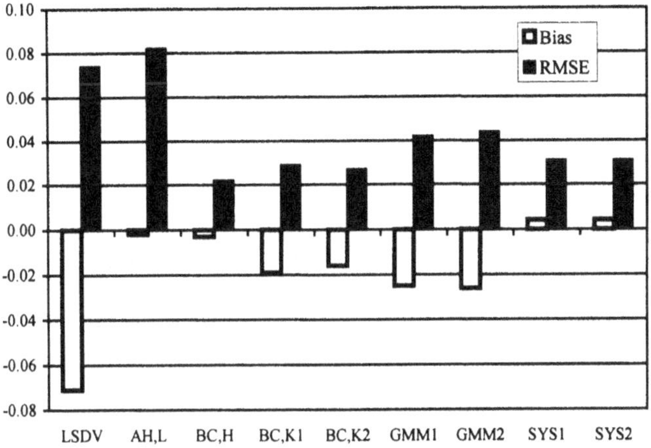

Fig. 3.2: Bias and Root Mean Square Error of β, N=100

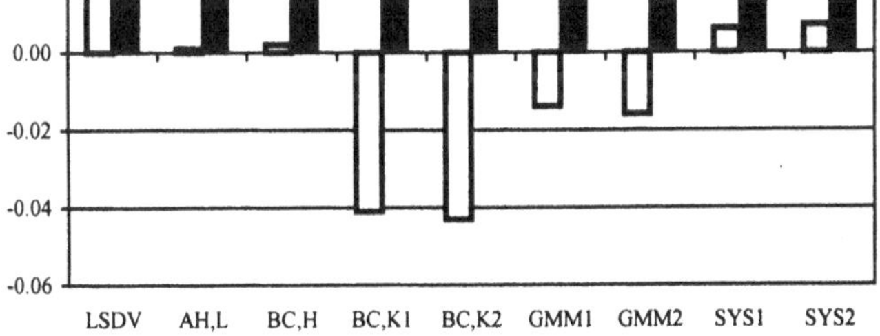

We find that in the simulation with 100 individuals the bias corrected estimator proposed by Hansen performed best according to the RMSE-criterion. The estimator is

4 The estimator proposed by Anderson and Hsiao making use of differences is clearly outperformed and not shown in the figures to ease comparability of the remaining estimators.

practically unbiased. The Anderson-Hsiao estimator using lagged levels as instruments is in average practically unbiased but according to the large standard deviation, rather inefficient. The system-estimator clearly outperforms the GMM estimator using only lagged levels as instrument. Quite surprisingly the bias corrected estimator proposed by Kiviet as well as the GMM estimators have a downward bias for the lagged endogenous variable as well as for the exogenous variable. Table 2 contains the simulation results for 1000 individuals.

Table 3.2: Simulation results, T=10, N=1000, $\sigma_\varepsilon^2 = 1$, $\rho = 0.5$, $\eta = 0.5$

	ρ				β			
	$\overline{X}$	$\overline{\hat{std}}$	std	$RMSE$	$\overline{X}$	$\overline{\hat{std}}$	std	$RMSE$
γ^{Pooled}	0.710	0.004	0.007	0.21	0.649	0.009	0.014	0.351
γ^{LSDV}	0.431	0.007	0.007	0.069	1.018	0.011	0.01	0.021
$\gamma^{AH,L}$	0.498	0.055	0.022	0.022	1.000	0.023	0.016	0.016
$\gamma^{AH,D}$	0.501	0.104	0.102	0.101	1.002	0.038	0.035	0.035
$\gamma^{BC,H}$	0.500	0.007	0.007	0.007	1.001	0.011	0.010	0.010
$\gamma^{BC,K1}$	0.480	0.007	0.007	0.021	0.961	0.011	0.010	0.040
$\gamma^{BC,K2}$	0.484	0.007	0.007	0.018	0.958	0.011	0.010	0.043
γ^{GMM1}	0.498	0.012	0.012	0.012	0.998	0.021	0.020	0.020
γ^{GMM2}	0.498	0.011	0.013	0.013	0.998	0.02	0.021	0.021
γ^{SYS1}	0.501	0.01	0.011	0.011	1.001	0.018	0.016	0.016
γ^{SYS2}	0.502	0.008	0.01	0.01	1.001	0.015	0.017	0.017

Fig. 3.3: Bias and Root Mean Square Error of ρ, N=1000

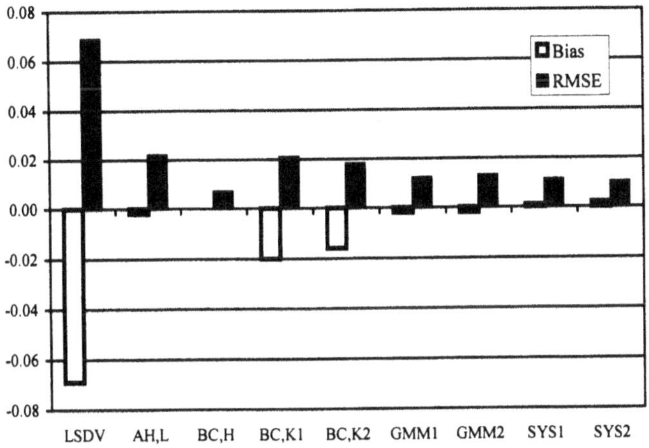

Fig. 3.4: Bias and Root Mean Square Error of β, N=1000

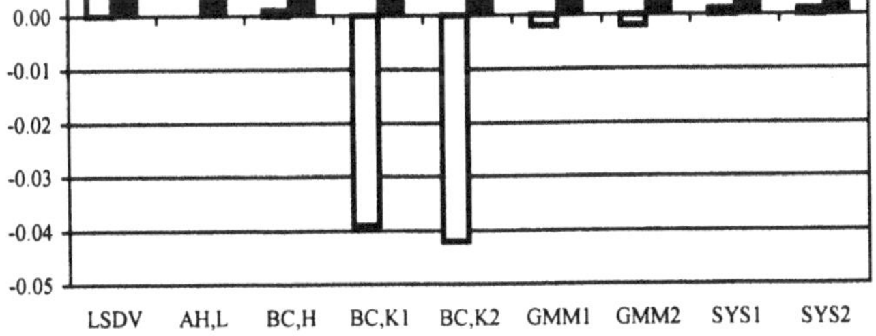

When comparing the simulation results for the case of 1000 individuals the results resemble but the GMM und system estimator improve considerably and perform better than the bias corrected estimators using the correction proposed by Kiviet. The improvement of the instrumented estimators of course had to be expected due to the well-known large sample properties of the GMM methods.

Now we turn to the assessment of the standard deviation of the estimators, which are important for statistical inference.

The following figure shows the comparison of the average estimated standard deviation and the empirical standard deviation of the simulation parameters.

Fig. 3.5: Measures of variation, ρ, N=1000

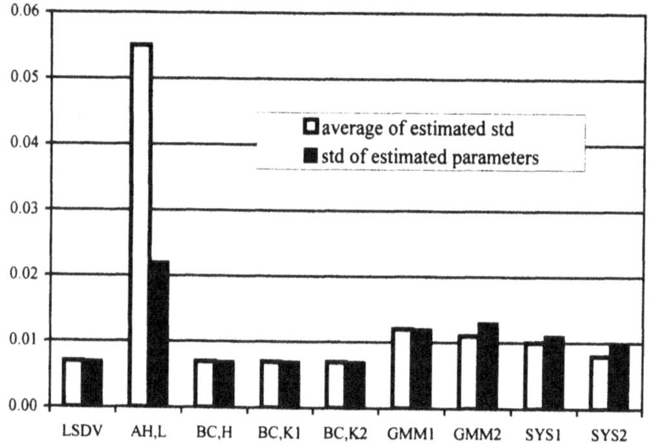

Fig. 3.6: Measures of variation, β, N=1000

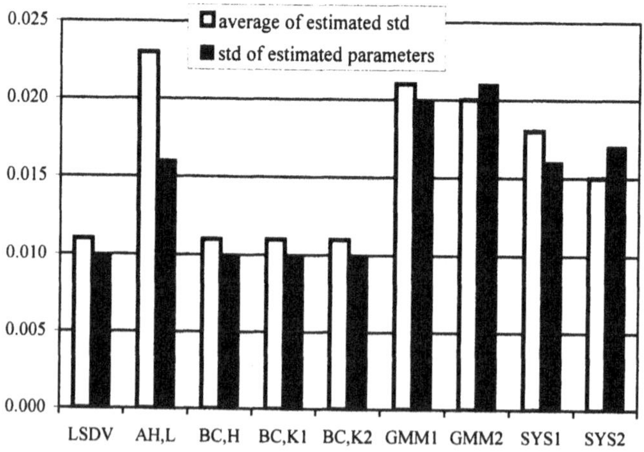

The diagrams show that the estimated standard deviation of the bias corrected estimators is very close to the empirical standard deviation of the estimators in the simulation runs. While the bias corrected estimators seem more efficient than the GMM estimators, the system-estimators are almost as efficient. But the results also demonstrate that the estimated standard deviations of the two step GMM and system estimators are strongly downward biased and not reliable.[5]

To sum up the results for the case of an exogenous regressor, we find that bias corrected methods, especially the method proposed by Hansen, seem superior. Especially for smaller samples the GMM and system estimators are less efficient, while the difference narrows when turning to large samples. When comparing the GMM estimator proposed by Arellano and Bond with the system estimator proposed by Blundell and Bond we find that the system estimator is superior, but both second step estimators making use of the estimated covariance matrix face the problem of unreliable standard errors.

3.3.2. The case of a predetermined endogenous explanatory variable

In this section we want to analyze the performance of the various estimators in the case of a predetermined endogenous explanatory variable x.

The simulation is based on the following model:

$$y_{it} = \rho\, y_{i,t-1} + \beta\, x_{it-1} + \alpha_i + \varepsilon_{it} \quad \text{where } \varepsilon_{it} \sim N(0,\sigma_\varepsilon^2) \text{ and } \alpha_i \sim N(0,1)$$

$$x_{it} = \eta\, x_{i,t-1} + \delta\, y_{it-1} + \zeta_i + \upsilon_{it} \quad \text{where } \upsilon_{it} \sim N(0,\sigma_\upsilon^2) \text{ and } \zeta_i \sim N(0,1)$$

While the instrumented estimators in this setting still are consistent due to the choice of instruments taking the predetermination into account the bias corrected estimators will become inconsistent. Because the bias corrected estimators proofed to be superior in the case of exogenous variables, we want to assess the trade off between the efficiency and the resulting bias. The adequate measure to take both into account is the RMSE-criterion.

---

5 See Windmeijer (2000) for a discussion of these fact and a proposed small sample correction for the standard deviation. For the case of 1000 individuals the small sample correction is neglectable.

Table 3.3: Simulation results, T=10, N=1000, $\sigma_\varepsilon^2 = 1$, $\sigma_\upsilon^2 = 1$, $\rho = 0.5$, $\eta = 0.5$, $\delta = 0.1$

	ρ				β			
	$\overline{X}$	$\overline{\hat{std}}$	std	RMSE	$\overline{X}$	$\overline{\hat{std}}$	std	RMSE
γ^{Pooled}	0.711	0.004	0.007	0.211	0.634	0.009	0.014	0.367
γ^{LSDV}	0.414	0.007	0.007	0.086	0.996	0.011	0.012	0.013
$\gamma^{AH,L}$	0.497	0.103	0.038	0.038	0.999	0.043	0.021	0.021
$\gamma^{AH,D}$	0.507	0.081	0.085	0.085	1.002	0.035	0.036	0.036
$\gamma^{BC,H}$	0.486	0.007	0.007	0.016	0.973	0.011	0.012	0.029
$\gamma^{BC,K1}$	0.463	0.007	0.007	0.038	0.941	0.011	0.011	0.060
$\gamma^{BC,K2}$	0.467	0.007	0.007	0.034	0.937	0.011	0.012	0.064
γ^{GMM1}	0.491	0.017	0.018	0.020	0.985	0.033	0.034	0.037
γ^{GMM2}	0.491	0.016	0.019	0.021	0.985	0.031	0.035	0.038
γ^{SYS1}	0.503	0.011	0.012	0.012	1.004	0.019	0.02	0.02
γ^{SYS2}	0.502	0.009	0.01	0.011	1.003	0.016	0.019	0.019

As could have been expected, in the case of predetermined endogenous explanatory variable, the simulation results are in favor of the instrumental variable estimators. The RMSE of the direct bias corrected estimator (BC,H) is about 50% larger than the system-estimator. Still the bias corrected estimator outperforms the GMM estimators and the estimators proposed by Anderson and Hsiao.

3.4. Conclusion

In this chapter we discussed several linear dynamic panel data estimators proposed in the literature. It is a well-known fact that the natural choice, the least squares dummy variable estimator is biased in the context of dynamic estimation. The estimators taking into account the resulting bias can be grouped broadly into the class of instrumental estimators and the class of direct bias corrected estimators. Because there are now various estimators available, the applied researcher faces the problem of choosing among them.

While in empirical applications instrumental estimators are widely used, simulation results seem to favor direct bias corrected methods. But to our knowledge there is no comparison of up to date instrumental estimators, like the system estimator proposed by Blundell and Bond (1998) and direct bias corrected methods (Kiviet 1995, Hansen 2001).

One special feature of the direct bias corrected methods is that they rely on the assumption of exogenous regressors. In the case of estimating investment functions based on balance sheet data, this assumption can be expected to be violated. The case of a predetermined but endogenous regressor is therefore also assessed by the means of Monte Carlo simulations.

The simulation results clearly favor the direct bias corrected estimators, especially the estimator proposed by Hansen (2001). The superiority of these estimators decreases with growing numbers of individuals in the simulation. This is the well-known fact of large sample properties of the GMM-methods. Turning to the case of endogenous predetermined regressors, the system-estimator proposed by Blundell and Bond is unbiased and most efficient, while direct bias corrected estimators perform similar to the GMM-estimator proposed by Arellano and Bond.

In the following empirical sections of our analysis we will apply the direct bias correction proposed by Hansen throughout. This decision is based on the performance of this estimator in the simulation as well as on the improved comparability of empirical results. Contrary to instrumental estimators, which for each function require a suitable set of valid instruments, the direct bias corrected estimator can be applied directly to the data set of interest. Knowing that the data set is very heterogeneous and mainly contains cross sectional information, the correlation between the variable we are interested in to analyze and the instrumented counterpart is in average as low as 0.02. Because of this week correlation with instruments the choice of instruments can have decisive effects of the final estimates. To preclude this possible source of instrumental testing is in our view the most convincing argument in favor of the direct bias estimation procedure.

4. The data source and measurement problems

In this chapter we first explain the data source, which the empirical analysis is based upon. In section 4.2. we discuss methods to overcome the problem of transforming depreciated balance sheet data of the capital stock at historical costs into economic meaningful capital stock figures at replacement costs, since this measure is a core figure in the calculation of Q. The problem of how to calculate Q based on firm level balance sheet data is discussed in section 4.3. We offer to competing measures of Q, one that is meant to mimic average Q based on stock market data as close as possible and another measure of Q, called marginal Q, that is based on forecasted marginal profitabilities of the firms capital stock.

4.1. The data source

The empirical analysis is based on the financial statements statistics of the Deutsche Bundesbank. This database covers about 50,000 to 70,000 enterprises each year, which represent about 4% of the total number of enterprises in Germany. In the context of its rediscount-lending operations the Bundesbank collects the financial statements of firms using trade bills to assess the creditworthiness of the bill-presenting firm.[1]

Because the sample is biased towards larger enterprises about 75% of the total turn over of the corporate sector in western Germany is covered. The time period covered by our sample is from 1987 to 1998.

The data set after calculating the capital stock using the detailed schedule of fixed asset movements leaves us with 3,359 firms and 11 years to start with including all sectors.

Especially the need to use the detailed schedule of fixed asset movements (Anlagespiegel) to apply our algorithm for calculating the capital stock at replacement costs shrinks the available considerably.

To prevent outliers biasing the results we drop the upper and lower 0.5 % of the observations of the following nine variables:

---

1 See Deutsche Bundesbank (1998) and Deutsche Bundesbank (1983, 1989, 1993, 1994). Stöss (2001) provides on overview of empirical research based on this data source.

- ratio of aggregated investment to the aggregated capital stock
- ratio of investment in equipment to the capital stock of equipment
- ratio of investment in structures to the capital stock of structures
- ratio of pre-tax profits to the capital stock
- ratio of sales to the capital stock
- ratio of cash flow to the capital stock
- ratio of operating income to the capital stock
- marginal Q
- average Q.

This leaves us with 1.315 manufacturing, 110 construction and 873 commerce, altogether 2,298 firms for the final analysis.

Table 4.1 contains the sectoral structure of the database used for final calculations:

Table 4.1: Sectoral distribution of firms

No.	Sector	n
1	Manufacture of food products and beverages	110
2	Manufacture of textiles	79
3	Manufacture of textile products	20
4	Manufacture of wood and wood products	82
5	Manufacture of pulp, paper and paper products	58
6	Publishing and Printing	44
7	Manufacture of chemicals and chemical products	87
8	Manufacture of rubber and plastic products	128
9	Manufacture of other non-metallic mineral products	106
10	Manufacture of basic metals	90
11	Manufacture of fabricated metal products, except machinery and equipment	127
12	Manufacture of machinery and equipment n.e.c.	237
13	Manufacture of electrical machinery and apparatus n.e.c., medical, precision and optical instruments	122
14	Manufacture of motor vehicles, trailers and semi-trailers	52
15	Construction	112
16	Wholesale trade and commission trade	562
17	Retail trade, Transport	298

Throughout the analysis we use all variables at nominal values. The reason for doing so is the use of ratios in the investment equation:

$$\widehat{\left(\frac{I}{K}\right)} = a_i + \beta_1 \left(\frac{I}{K}\right)_{-1} + \beta_2\, Q_{i,t-1} + \beta_3 \left(\frac{S}{K}\right)_{-1} + \beta_4 \left(\frac{CF}{K}\right)_{-1}$$

By dividing through the capital stock the resulting ratios contain the relevant information for the investor according to our understanding. We do not see a ratio of e.g. Sales in prices of year *t-k* to the capital stock at prices of year *t-k* as relevant information to the investor. With the same reasoning we do not see an investor deciding about investment in prices of year *t-k* divided by the capital stock at prices of year *t-k*.

The use of nominal values has practical reasons as well. There is neither firm level price information to deflate the nominal values nor have all variables (think about the cash flow) the structure of a product of prices times quantities. Therefore the use of constant prices might lead to unreasonable figures and misleading results. Because firm level price data are not available one might think about using sectoral price information, which for some of the variables are available. This procedure could only be applied to some of the variables (I, K) and not for others (CF, market value of the capital stock).

Therefore one way could be seen in the use of an economy wide price measure e.g. the price index of final national uses to prevent trends in the data purely from increasing price levels. Of course for the ratios this price indices would cancel out. The only variable we use in real values is the balance sheet total as a measure for firm size. Here we use the price index of final national uses.

Starting with a very large data set the number of observations decreases considerably through incomplete balance sheets, outlier control and balancing.

4.2. The capital stock at replacement costs: A new algorithm

The most prominent approaches for this transformation are the ones proposed by Lindenberg/Ross (1981), the NBER-approach (Hall et al. (1988)) and the algorithm suggested by Lewellen/Badrinath (1997). In this paper we suggest an alternative algorithm, which, according to our understanding and the results of a comparison based on Monte Carlo simulations, is almost comparable to the precise results of the algorithm by Lewellen and Badrinath but has considerable lower data requirements.

In the following section we sketch the aforementioned approaches and try to show the core idea as well as the data requirements for the implementation, before we present our own approach. The next section contains a Monte Carlo simulation intended to compare the outcomes of the different approaches with our own suggested algorithm.

4.2.1. A short review of the literature

4.2.1.1. The approach by Lindenberg und Ross

The algorithm by Lindenberg and Ross (1991) starts from year $t = 1$ where the book value at historical costs less accumulated depreciation is taken as an approximation for the unknown net capital stock at replacement values. At the beginning of period $t = 1$ we have (in the following K^* denotes capital stock at replacement costs while K denotes the book value)

$$K_t^* = K_t .$$

In the following periods the capital stock is updated taking into account the depreciation rate (δ, book rate), price changes (i) and the technical process (θ) as well as gross investment (I_t):

$$K_t^* = K_{t-1}^* \frac{(1+i)(1-\delta)}{(1+\theta)} + I_t .$$

The capital stock contains fixed assets as well as inventories. The procedure described above is applied to fixed assets. With respect to inventories two cases are distinguished:

- When using FIFO (First-In-First-Out) the valuation of the stock is rather close to replacement costs and the book values remain unadjusted.

- When using LIFO (Last-In-First-Out) greater discrepancies will occur. In this case the book values of inventories will be adjusted using a procedure close to the one described above and the parameter settings $\delta = 0$ and $\theta = 0$.

4.2.1.2. "NBER-approach" by Hall et al.

While inventories are treated with a technique similar to the approach of Lindenberg and Ross the NBER-approach (1988) adjusts the book value of fixed assets for price changes.[2] Central to the algorithm is the assumption about the average age $\bar{a}$ of the existing capital stock. Thus if $\bar{a}$=4, the adjustment of the book value takes into account

---

2 This approach is based on the algorithm proposed by Salinger and Summers (1983).

the price changes of capital goods, π, for the last 4 years. In general the estimated capital stock in period t is given by

$$K_t^* = K_t \prod_{j=1}^{\bar{a}} (1+\pi_{t-j+1}).$$

It is evident that the quality of the estimation hinges on the correctness of $\bar{a}$. The average age is calculated using historical balance sheet data for depreciation D:

(1) Calculation of average age in period t:

$$a_t = \frac{\sum_{\tau=1}^{t} D_\tau}{D_t}.$$

(2) The average lifetime n_t for capital goods in period t is given by:

$$n_t = \frac{K_t^g}{D_t},$$

where K_t^g denotes the gross capital stock (no depreciation subtracted) at historical costs in period t.

(3) The estimated lifetimes are smoothed over five periods:

$$n_t^* = \frac{1}{5} \sum_{j=0}^{4} n_{t-j}.$$

(4) The final estimate of the average age is given by adjusting the preliminary estimate a_t with the ratio of smoothed lifetime to lifetime calculated for period t:

$$\bar{a} = a_t \frac{n_t^*}{n_t}.$$

4.2.1.3. The approach by Lewellen and Badrinath

Compared to the two algorithms described above, the approach suggested by Lewellen and Badrinath (1997) is more complex. The basic idea is to disaggregate the actual capital stock into the years of purchase in the first step and the price adjustment for the different vintages in the second step. Like the $\bar{a}$ in the NBER-approach, this approach contains a magical number as well. This time the key number for the quality of the procedure's results is the longest lifetime of capital goods $\tilde{n}$. Assuming that number is correct, the actual capital stock contains investment goods of the last $\tilde{n}$ vintages I_t:

$$K_t^g = \sum_{\tau=t}^{t-(\tilde{n}-1)} I_\tau .$$

To estimate $\tilde{n}$ we start with $\tilde{n} = 1$ and increase $\tilde{n}$ until the following inequality holds:

$$\sum_{\tau=t}^{t-(\tilde{n}-1)} I_\tau \leq K_t^g < \sum_{\tau=t}^{t-\tilde{n}} I_\tau .$$

If

$$\sum_{\tau=t}^{t-(\tilde{n}-1)} I_\tau < K_t^g ,$$

the difference between cumulative investment and the gross capital stock at historical costs

$$K_t^g - \sum_{\tau=t}^{t-(\tilde{n}-1)} I_\tau > 0$$

is added to the oldest still-living vintage of investment.

Now we are interested in the share $\tilde{g}_\tau$ of the vintage I_τ that is still contained (not fully depreciated) in period t. Given the period of purchase τ under the assumption of linear depreciation for $\tilde{n}$ periods, the still-living share of the vintage is given as

$$\tilde{g}_\tau = \frac{2\tilde{n} - 2(t-\tau) - 1}{2\tilde{n}}, \quad \tau = t - \tilde{n} + 1, ..., t .$$

Summing the parts, the replacement value of the net capital stock for period t (starting point) can be estimated as:

$$K_t^* = \sum_{\tau=t}^{t-(\tilde{n}-1)} I_\tau \tilde{g}_\tau \frac{P_t}{P_\tau} .$$

Adjustment routines

The algorithm leads to estimates of cumulative depreciations of the capital goods, which are still contained in the capital stock. These estimates DK_t^* might differ from the book values of cumulative depreciations DK_t. This possible discrepancy will be eliminated via the following adjustment routine.

The estimates of cumulative depreciations of still-living capital goods are given by

$$DK_t^* = \sum_{\tau=t}^{t-(\tilde{n}-1)} I_\tau (1-\tilde{g}_\tau).$$

These estimates are contrasted with the book value of cumulative depreciations of still-living goods:

$$DK_t = K_t^g - K_t .$$

If we have

$$DK_t > DK_t^* ,$$

the difference

$$DK_t - DK_t^* ,$$

will be added to the oldest vintage still living.

If we have

$$DK_t < DK_t^* ,$$

all estimated depreciations will be adjusted (diminished) by the following ratio:

$$\frac{DK_t}{DK_t^*} .$$

This adjustment routine guarantees the equality of estimated and balance sheet data for the net capital stock at historical costs.

4.2.1.4. Critique

The Lindenberg-Ross-approach is rather simple and easy to implement. But it is obvious that the quality of the estimated capital stock at actual prices will increase over time. The quality of the initial estimate will be rather poor owing to overly fast depreciation of book values because of tax considerations and the neglecting of capital goods price changes. The updating of the capital stock might also be biased because book depreciation rates probably overstate economic depreciation rates. Our own empirical estimates will show that initially the book value amounts on average to only 40% of the economically meaningful replacement value.[3]

As in the approach taken by Lindenberg and Ross, in the NBER-approach it is assumed that book depreciations equal economic depreciations. Especially for German accounting data, there will be major discrepancies because in general the tax-oriented depreciation rates will exceed the economic rates. The calculations of average age and average lifetime ignore the fact that the stock of fixed assets in a period t is a composition of several investment vintages.

The approach taken by Lewellen and Badrinath is by far the most complex of the three discussed. By taking into account the age structure of the still-living capital stock, the price adjustment can be expected to be rather precise. The main disadvantage of this approach can be seen in the rather high data requirements. To estimate the capital stock for period t the investment data for the $\tilde{n}$-1 years preceding year t have to be given. Taking into consideration the rather long lifetime of structures, these data requirements will hardly ever be met when working with micro balance sheet data. Finally, the assumption of an equal lifetime of all capital goods seems to be rather oversimplifying.

4.2.2. A new algorithm

4.2.2.1. The basic idea

The basic idea of the new algorithm, which we propose, is to split the actual capital stock into two additive components. The first component contains the vintages, which

---

3 One solution often applied in empirical work is to leave out several years at the beginning of the period covered. While that avoids using the worst estimates at the beginning of the estimation period, there will still be a strongly decreasing measurement error over time.

are still alive and already belonged to the capital stock at the beginning of the first year in the data set. We will add the subscript "old" to indicate this component. (In our data set this was the year 1987.) The second component consists of the capital goods, which were acquired during the years covered by the data set, and still belongs to the capital stock. This component will be indicated by the subscript "new". For these two components we apply different adjustment procedures to transform the book values at historical costs and tax-driven depreciations into economically meaningful net capital stock figures at replacement costs. The final estimate of the capital stock will therefore be

$$K_t^* = K_{old,t}^* + K_{new,t}^* .$$

Let us first consider the "new" component. For this component the investment at actual prices for period t is covered in the available data set. Each vintage leaves the capital stock according to the retirement function commonly employed in the classical perpetual-inventory procedure. In addition, each year the capital stock is revalued so as to take account of the price development of capital goods.

Now let us look at the "old" part of the capital stock. The crucial point is to disaggregate the existing capital stock at the beginning of the first year covered by the data set t_0 into its vintages. If this is achieved in a plausible way, each vintage leaves the capital stock in line with the retirement function in the same way as the vintages of the "new" capital stock.

Besides this disaggregation into the different vintages, a second disaggregation is the important separation into structures and equipment. These two components are characterized by very different lifetimes, which are associated with very different depreciations as well as different price changes.

As the depreciations given in the balance sheet data are mainly driven by tax considerations, their use would lead to a severe underestimation of the lifetime of capital goods. Therefore we use sectoral data for depreciation rates and capital goods' lifetimes, which we assume, will be closer to economic reality. Since the data set does not contain any price information, we also use sectoral price data. Both sectoral data sets are disaggregated into structures and equipment. The inventories are not revalued. Given that most firms employ the First-In-First-Out valuation scheme, we take the book values as being sufficiently close to replacement values. In this case (FIFO) there will only be minor differences between book values and replacement values. In the next section of the paper we will formalize the algorithm and present further details.

4.2.2.2. The disaggregation of the first period's capital stock into different vintages

The detailed schedule of fixed asset movements (Anlagenspiegel) contains information concerning the sum of all past investment still in stock at historical costs (gross capital stock at historical costs, K_t^g).

Disaggregation into structures and equipment

In our starting period t_0 we disaggregate the value of the capital stock ($K_{t_0}^g$) into structures and equipment based on the respective shares of structures and equipment in the balance sheets:

$$K_{t_0}^{g,j} = K_{t_0}^g \cdot \frac{K_{t_0}^j}{K_{t_0}}, \quad j\text{=1,2 (structures, equipment),}$$

with:

$K_{t_0}^{g,j}$ accumulated still-living investment at historical costs, type j

$K_{t_0}^g$ accumulated still-living investment at historical costs (Anlagenspiegel), aggregate

$K_{t_0}^j$ net capital stock at historical costs (balance sheet), type j

K_{t_0} net capital stock at historical costs (balance sheet), aggregate

In the following all calculations are performed at the disaggregated level for structures and equipment separately. To improve readability we leave out the subscript j.

Sectoral adjustment in year t_0

We do not make the counterfactual assumption of equality between historical cost data and actual replacement values. This procedure would lead to a severe underestimation of the net capital stock at actual replacement values. Instead we use sectoral data supplied by the Federal Statistical Office (Statistisches Bundesamt) to adjust for the discrepancies stemming from the different depreciation methods and price schemes.

The starting point is the firm level balance sheet value adjusted for the sectoral ratio for year t_0:

$$K_{t_0}^{*} = K_{t_0}^{g} \cdot \frac{K_{t_0}^{r,s}}{K_{t_0}^{g,h,s}},$$

$K_{t_0}^{g,h,s}$ gross capital stock at historical costs in sector s,

$K_{t_0}^{r,s}$ net capital stock at replacement values in sector s

Adjustment takes into account the different price scheme as well as the difference between gross and net capital stock. It is obvious that the adjusted values in the initial year t_0 will be the closer to the true value the more the structure of firm i's capital stock resembles the structure of the capital stock in sector s in terms of both goods and age.

4.2.2.3. The retirement of the investment vintages

We disaggregate a vintage t into parts of different lifetime n. α_n denotes the part of a vintage with lifetime n (it retires after being n years in stock) and N is the maximum lifetime. In the course of its maximum lifetime N the vintage will retire completely. Therefore we have

$$\sum_{n=1}^{N} \alpha_n = 1$$

and

$$I_t = \sum_{n=1}^{N} I_t \alpha_n .$$

For determining the retirement ratios α_n we use the gamma function, which is also used by the Federal Statistical Office:

$$\alpha_n = \alpha(\overline{n}, n) = \frac{9^9}{\overline{n}^9 \cdot 8!} \cdot n^8 \cdot e^{\frac{-9 \cdot n}{\overline{n}}}.$$

This gamma function tells us which part of a fixed asset with average lifetime $\overline{n}$ retires at the age of n years.

Fig. 4.1: The retirement function for average lifetimes of 5 and 10 years

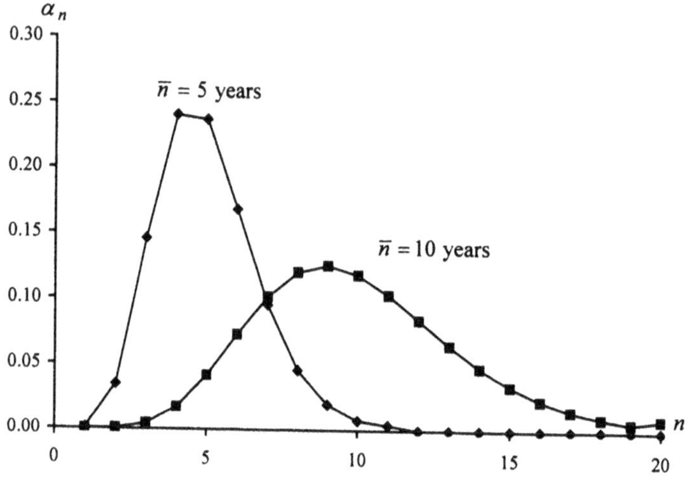

For the individual firm i the average lifetime $\overline{n}$ of the sector the firm belongs to is used.[4] It is worth noting at this point that average lifetimes for structures and equipment differ considerably. These will be taken into account at the sectoral level.

In the next step we calculate linear depreciations of the vintage $\tau \geq t_0$ in period k:

$$D_{\tau,k} = I_\tau \cdot \sum_{n=1}^{N} \alpha_n \delta_{j,n} ,$$

4 Attempts to estimate the average lifetime for firm i individually would require very long time series, especially for structures, which usually will not be available in micro panel data sets.

with

n lifetime

N maximum lifetime

j age (=k-τ+1) of vintage τ in period k

$\delta_{j,n}$ depreciation rate, taking the half-year rule into account (hence we assume fixed assets join the firm in the middle of the year)

$$\delta_{j,n} = \begin{cases} \frac{0{,}5}{n} & \text{if } j = 1 \\ \frac{1}{n} & \text{if } 1 < j \leq n \\ \frac{0{,}5}{n} & \text{if } j = n+1 \\ 0 & \text{if } j > n+1 \end{cases}$$

Accumulating these depreciations from starting period t_0 until actual period t results in

$$DK_{\tau,t} = \sum_{k=\tau}^{t} D_{\tau,k} = \sum_{k=\tau}^{t} I_\tau \cdot \sum_{n=1}^{N} \alpha_n \delta_{j,n}\,, \quad j = k\text{-}\tau\text{+}1.$$

The price changes will be taken into consideration by using sectoral price indices P_t/P_τ where period t is the actual year and τ is the year the investment took place.

The replacement value of the capital stock less depreciation at the beginning of period t is the sum of the still-living investment adjusted for price changes:

$$K^*_{new,t} = \sum_{\tau=t_0}^{t} \left(I_\tau - DK_{\tau,t}\right)\frac{P_t}{P_\tau}.$$

4.2.2.4. Disaggregation of the capital stock at the beginning of the initial year into its vintages and retirements

The initial estimate of the capital stock is disaggregated into its vintages of investment separately for structures and equipment. To achieve this disaggregation several assumptions are necessary:

- the retirement function is stable over time,

- investment in the prior years has taken place evenly,
- the capital goods depreciate linearly over time.

These assumptions imply:

- what shares of investment vintages still belong to the capital stock, and
- the average lifetime of the vintages.

Let us denote the oldest vintage still belonging to the capital stock with τ_0. Then summing the depreciations and taking into account the price adjustment $P_t / P_{t_0 -1}$ we obtain the replacement value less depreciation of the capital goods still living in year t_0 at the end of year t:

$$K^{*}_{old,t} = \left(K^{*}_{old,t_0 -1} - \sum_{\tau = t_0 - N}^{t_0 -1} DK^{old}_{\tau,t} \right) \frac{P_t}{P_{t_0 -1}} .$$

The calculation of the depreciations

The counterpart to the retirement function is the survival function. This function tells us which part of the fixed asset is not retired yet at its age of n years:

$$g_n = \begin{cases} 1 & \text{if } n = 1 \\ g_{n-1} - a_{n-1} & \text{if } n > 1 \end{cases} .$$

Using the survival function, the age structure of the gross capital stock at the beginning of the initial year t_0 (or at the end of year $t_0 - 1$) can be derived.

Let

$$G = \sum_{n=1}^{N} g_n ,$$

then the share of the gross capital stock at the end of period $t_0 - 1$ from investment taking place at year $\tau < t_0$ with age $j = t_0 - \tau$ is given by

$$\frac{g_j}{G} .$$

Hence the total value of investment vintage $\tau < t_0$ still alive in the period $t_0 - 1$ at replacement costs of the year $t_0 - 1$ can be estimated as

$$K^*_{t_0-1,\tau} = K^*_{t_0-1} \cdot \frac{g_{t_0-\tau}}{G}.$$

Since

$$\frac{g_j}{G} = \frac{\alpha_j + \alpha_{j+1} + \ldots + \alpha_N}{G}$$

this figure can be disaggregated into fractions with different lifetimes j:

$$K^*_{t_0-1,\tau} = \frac{K^*_{t_0-1}}{G} \cdot \sum_{j=t_0-\tau}^{N} \alpha_j .$$

The depreciations of vintage $\tau < t_0$ in period k are

$$D^{old}_{\tau,k} = \frac{K^*_{t_0-1}}{G} \cdot \sum_{n=1}^{N} \alpha_n \delta_{j,n} ,$$

$j = k\text{-}\tau\text{+}1$ age of vintage τ in period k.

The cumulative depreciations of vintage $\tau < t_0$ from starting period t_0 until actual period t are

$$DK^{old}_{\tau,t} = \sum_{k=\tau}^{t} D^{old}_{\tau,k} = \sum_{k=\tau}^{t} \frac{K^*_{t_0-1}}{G} \cdot \sum_{n=1}^{N} \alpha_n \delta_{j,n} , \quad j = k\text{-}\tau\text{+}1.$$

These estimated depreciations are valued at replacement costs of the year $t_0 - 1$. The final adjustment using the price relation P_t / P_{t_0-1} leads to the estimation at replacement costs of year t.

4.2.3. A comparison of the different approaches

In this section of the paper we run a Monte-Carlo simulation to assess the performance of the algorithms by Lindenberg/Ross, the NBER approach, the algorithm proposed by Lewellen/Badrinath and our own proposed alternative algorithm.

- The average lifetime $\bar{n}$ of fixed assets is 10 years, evenly distributed between 5 and 15 years.
- Each firm has a specific average lifetime $\bar{n}_i$ of its fixed assets and a specific retirement function.
- The retirement rates α_{in} of fixed assets with lifetimes $n = 5, 6, ..., 15$ for firm i are drawn at random. They will be held constant over the whole simulation period. The average lifetime of the firm's fixed assets is then given by

$$\bar{n}_i = \sum_{n=5}^{15} n \cdot \alpha_{in} .$$

- We set book depreciations equal to economic depreciations, so there is no need to correct non-economic, tax-oriented depreciations. (Note that this assumption has to be made in the approaches by L/R, NBER and L/W, while in our algorithm we make use of an adjustment procedure in the initial year to correct for differences and apply an economic meaningful linear depreciation scheme.)

A. Equal investment throughout all years, price increases randomly drawn from a uniform distribution between 0 and 10 % per year.

B. Random draws from the empirical data (Bilanzstatistik/VGR)

According to this procedure, the true capital stock at replacement values is generated for a period of 70 years. We assume that the data available to the researcher start at period 21 ($=t_0$).

Fig. 4.2: Distribution of errors for the different algorithms (estimation period 30 to 50, age of firms at initial estimation is 20 years, 1000 firms)

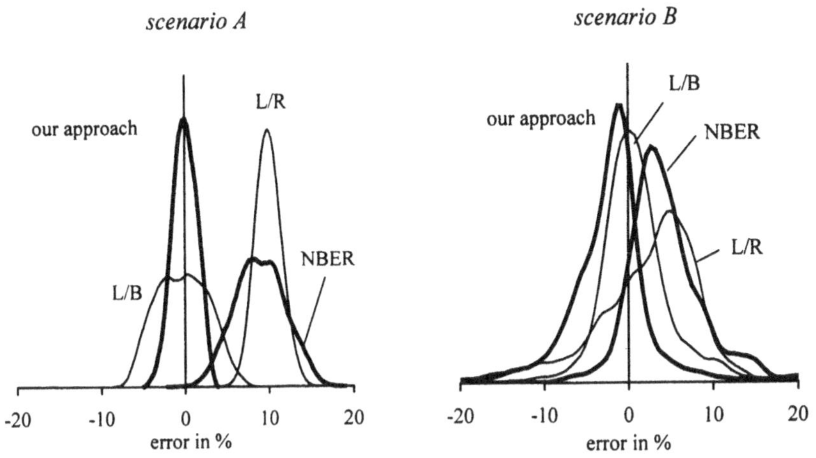

Notes: L/R = Lindenberg and Ross, L/B = Lewellen/Badrinath. We use kernel-density estimates (triangular kernel, bandwidth 1 %).

It can be seen from the simulation results that the algorithm we propose performs rather well. The results show that the algorithm suggested by Lewellen/Baldrinath outperforms our algorithm. But it should be remembered that their approach requires investment to be known at least 10 years before the first capital stock can be calculated. Therefore their approach, even having the smallest error, cannot be applied in most empirical cases. Comparing the algorithm, which we propose with the two approaches having similar data requirements, we find that the errors for the new algorithm are rather small.

4.2.4. Estimates of the capital stock

4.2.4.1. The aggregate capital stock at replacement costs

If we summarize the results, we find that the ratio of the aggregate capital stock at replacement costs to the corresponding balance sheet values at historical costs is on average 2.6. The comparison of the mean and the median shows that the distribution is extremely skewed, the median is just above an eighth of the mean.

Table 4.2: Balance sheet figures and estimates of the capital stock, Mill. DM

		n	$\overline{X}$	σ	*Median*	$Q_{75\%}$-$Q_{25\%}$
All	Balance sheet	23,140	32.93	233.94	4.36	12.10
	Estimated		85.49	633.83	10.46	28.56
Manufacturing	Balance sheet	13,420	48.11	303.05	7.22	17.78
	Estimated		126.63	821.61	17.38	43.92
Construction	Balance sheet	1,120	21.12	54.35	4.28	15.23
	Estimated		55.08	151.03	9.75	32.89
Commerce	Balance sheet	8,600	10.77	51.93	1.80	4.56
	Estimated		25.26	135.09	4.25	10.97

There is a strong increase in the capital stock at replacement values by about 40% between 1988 and 1993. In the following years up to 1998 the capital stock is almost stationary.

Fig. 4.3: Sum of calculated capital stocks at replacement values

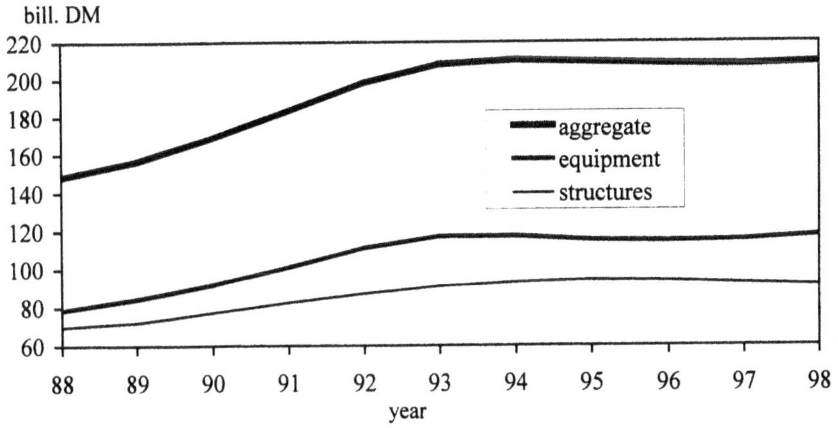

If we estimate median and quartiles it is apparent that the distribution of the capital stocks of individual firms is extraordinary skewed. The median of the capital stock in our database is about 10 million DM.

Fig. 4.4: Level and dispersion of the aggregate capital stocks

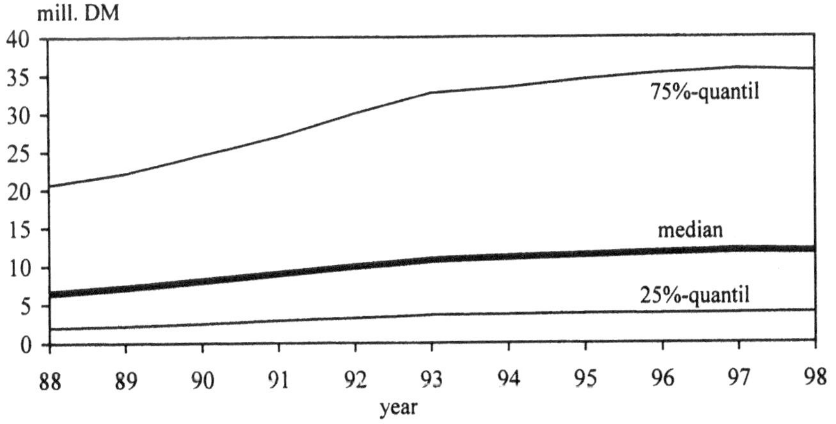

To compare the time series of the capital stock in the three main sectors manufacturing, construction and commerce we show the ratio of the actual capital stock to the figure in 1988. While we observe a permanent growth of the capital stock in the sector commerce, the capital stock in the sector construction is sharply decreasing since 1996. The capital stock in manufacturing reached its peak already in 1994. After three years of decreasing capital stock it was slowly growing in 1997 but is still below its 1994 value.

Fig. 4.5: Sectoral capital stocks, 1988=100

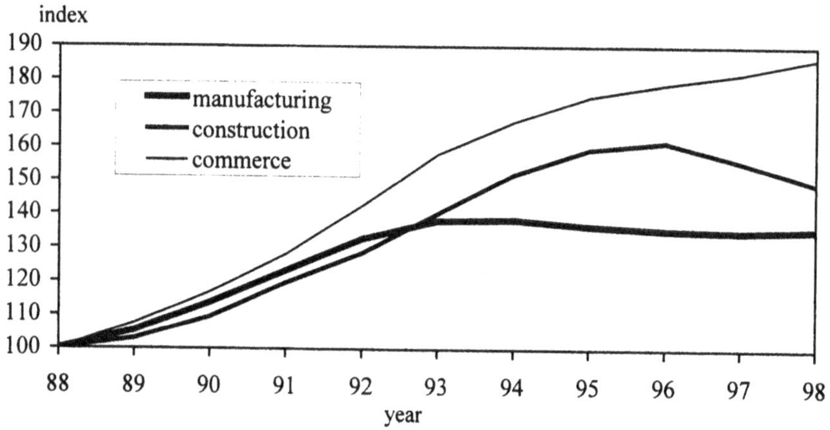

4.2.4.2. A comparison with official sectoral data

For calculating sectoral capital stocks based on the individual balance sheet data, we expand the sectoral estimates proportionally by the ratio of the sum of sales to the sectoral sales figures.

The comparison with official sectoral data (national accounts) shows that for manufacturing and construction the estimates based on the individual balance sheet data resemble the aggregate data reasonably well. Only for the wholesale/retail trade sector do the balance sheet-based figures underestimate the sectoral data noticeably. When assessing the results it should be borne in mind that no information concerning the sectoral level of capital stocks was used in the calculations. Only sectoral price changes and sectoral ratios of different price concepts were used for adjusting the book values as well as the sales coverage ratio of our database. We therefore conclude that the algorithm used for estimating the capital stock at replacement values based on given historical cost data from firm-level balance sheets performs rather well.

Fig. 4.6: Estimates by proportional expansion through sales

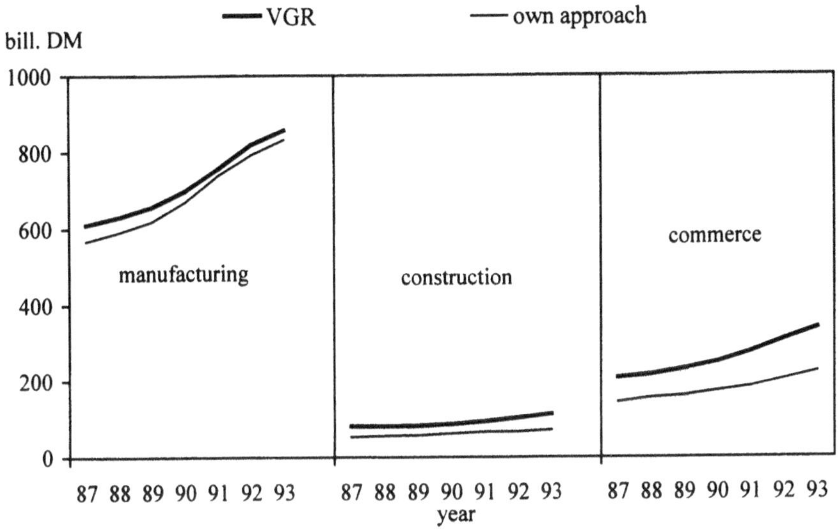

4.3. The Calculation of *Q*

While the advantage of average *Q* (Q^a) based on stock prices is the exploitation of market expectations there are several serious drawbacks to this conventional approach. First, market expectations can be rather poor. The recent slump in technology shares, which lost about 90% of their value within one year, may serve as an example of the noisiness of share prices.[5] The second drawback is that only a small fraction of an economy's firms is quoted on stock markets. Finally, it is marginal *Q* (Q^m) that is theoretically relevant for the firm's investment decision and not average *Q*, except under special conditions concerning the production technology.

In this chapter we outline our approach to calculating measures of *Q* using balance sheet data.[6] Both measures of *Q* we calculate are based on balance sheet data using a vector-autoregressive forecasting procedure. By estimating market values of equity, we first calculate average *Q* values comparable to the conventional *Q* measures based on stock markets. In a second approach following Gilchrist and Himmelberg (1995, 1998) we estimate marginal *Q* values based on strong assumptions about firms' production technology. After giving a brief overview of related work, the estimation procedures as well as empirical results are presented.

4.3.1. An Overview of empirical work using the direct forecasting approach

In the following overview we concentrate on empirical papers that adopt the direct forecasting approach. An extensive overview of empirical studies using stock market data was already provided by Hubbard (1998). We start with the influential paper by Abel and Blanchard (1986), which introduced the method of vector autoregression into the context of *Q*-models. Even though it only used aggregated data, the paper laid the fundamental basis for the following extensions to panel data by Gilchrist and Himmelberg (1995, 1998). The paper by Bontempi et al (2001) follows Gilchrist and Himmelberg by applying the approach to a large panel data set of non-quoted Italian firms.

---

5 See for a discussion of bubbles and fundamentals Chirinko/Schaller (1996).

6 See Ciccolo/Fromm (1980) for a discussion of balance sheet information in the context of the *Q*-theory.

4.3.1.1. The approach of Abel and Blanchard

Abel and Blanchard base their approach on the *Q*-theory of investment. Instead of using the conventional stock market-based average *Q*, they estimate *Q* through forming expectations on future returns based on lagged variables.[7] The authors use a VAR model to make use of the time series information contained in their macroeconomic data set. Marginal *Q* is estimated as the discounted sum of expected future profits.[8] The expectations of the unknown marginal profits and the unknown discount factors are each estimated as linear combinations of an observable vector *Z* which evolves according to a vector-autoregressive process. As the information set Ω_{t-1} includes only lagged values of *Z*, the estimated Q^m is a beginning-of-period marginal profit of investment.[9]

Variables used to estimate the VAR are, besides the returns on equity and debt, the ratio of labor cost to the capital stock, the sales/capital stock ratio, the stock market valuation of capital, average *Q*, the manufacturing price inflation, and the investment ratio.

In the estimated investment functions, only lagged values of the estimated marginal *Q* series have any explanatory power for investment, whereas the parameter of current Q^m is insignificantly negative. If added to the investment equation, lagged sales appear to have a significant positive influence on investment.

The performance of marginal *Q* in explaining the investment ratio is relatively poor. The authors present a list of possible causes of the poor results: the aggregation problems, the assumption of homogeneity of capital, the assumption of perfect capital markets and the negligence of liquidity constraints.

---

7 See Abel/Blanchard (1986), p. 249.

8 Thereby Abel and Blanchard treat the future discount rate as an unknown random variable. In this case the estimation of the unknown marginal *Q* requires taking into account the product of random variables.

9 Abel and Blanchard use quarterly data on US manufacturing for the period 1948:2 to 1979:3. The VAR model is estimated using 5 or 7 variables following a fourth-order vector-autoregressive process.

4.3.1.2. The extension by Gilchrist and Himmelberg

Following Abel and Blanchard (1986), Gilchrist and Himmelberg estimate a set of vector-autoregressive forecasting equations using a subset of balance sheet information. The forecasts of the VAR model are used to construct the expected value of marginal Q conditional on the observed fundamentals. The expected value of marginal Q is called fundamental Q.[10]

The unobservable marginal profit of capital is proxied by a measure of realized profits in relation to the existing capital. This approximation holds under strong assumptions concerning the production technology.[11]

The VAR model is estimated separately for a priori liquidity constrained and unconstrained firms to allow for differences in the forecasting scheme. The authors do not use firm-specific depreciation rates or time-varying interest rates. The fixed value assumed for depreciation is 15% and the fixed value assumed for the interest rate is 6%.

Tobin's Q, an estimate of average Q, based on share prices leads to much lower parameter estimates compared to fundamental Q. Adding cash flow as a further explanatory variable leads to a significant cash flow sensitivity for both Q specifications. When the sample is grouped a priori, only the constrained firms show significant cash flow sensitivity. Controlling for cash flow through the incorporation in the forecasting system does not alter the findings of the previous literature.

Even if the authors find Tobin's Q a poor proxy for investment opportunities, the results of the literature using Tobin's Q are confirmed. The fundamental Q seems to be superior, leading to higher parameter estimates. Because cash flow is explicitly included in the forecasting model, the authors interpret an additional sensitivity of cash flow as evidence of the existence of capital market imperfections.

---

10 In the 1998 paper Gilchrist and Himmelberg extend the approach, analyzing in a first step the dynamics of firms' investment behaviour using a VAR model for panel data. See Gilchrist/Himmelberg (1998).

11 See Gilchrist/Himmelberg (1995), p. 550.

4.3.1.3. The distinction between equipment and structures

Bontempi et al base their analysis on the fundamental distinction between equipment and structures.[12] These two components of the capital stock are characterized by different rates of depreciation and a different tax treatment. The usual aggregation of equipment and structures is criticized because this aggregation rests on the counterfactual assumption of perfect substitutability. Further, the authors assume that equipment and structures show different adjustment costs.[13]

The results show that equipment reacts strongly and significantly to marginal *Q*, whereas structures do not respond to marginal *Q*.[14] Some of the regressions have to be interpreted with care because tests question the validity of the instruments. When testing for different forms of adjustment costs, the authors find that the assumption of convex adjustment costs does not hold for structures. This implies a fixed component in the adjustment costs. When estimating separate equations for purchases and sales of investment goods, the results show that only equipment responds significantly to marginal *Q*, with purchases reacting much more strongly than sales.

In a further step Bontempi et al explore the possibility of interrelated adjustment costs. It is therefore assumed that the level of structures influences the adjustment costs of equipment and vice versa, and that the adjustment cost function is linearly homogeneous. The estimated investment functions now include, besides the *Q*-measures for equipment and structures, the ratio of the two components of the capital stock as well as the product of *Q* and the measure of the capital stock's structure. For this investment equations *Q* is significant for structures as well as for equipment, while the structure of the capital stock is never significant and the combined effect only sometimes.[15]

---

12 See Bontempi et al. (2001), p. 2.

13 The authors use a large database including balance sheets and income statements of more than 52,000 Italian manufacturing firms. The final estimates are base on a balanced panel of 1,539 firms.

14 See Bontempi et al. (2001), p. 16.

15 See Bontempi et al. (2001), p. 23.

4.3.2. The Calculation of Q using firm-level balance sheet data

We use the following definition of marginal Q stated by Hayashi (1982) as the starting point: "... marginal Q, is the ratio of the market value of an additional unit of capital to its replacement cost."[16]

As marginal Q is not observed, one way to overcome this problem followed extensively in the empirical literature is to use stock market data to measure unobservable expectations. Since in Germany only the smallest share of an economy's firms is quoted on stock markets, the concept of using stock market data to study firms' investment behavior excludes the majority of firms from an empirical investigation.[17] When using accounting data it is therefore necessary to apply alternative concepts to find measures that proxy for the expectations about future profits or future marginal profitabilities of capital. In the following we apply two concepts for measuring the firm's investment profitabilities, average Q and marginal Q.

4.3.3. Calculating Tobin's Q (average Q)

The approach used in this paper is based on the formula used by several authors[18] to calculate Tobin's Q (Q^a) for firm i at period t as the ratio of the market value of equity (V_{it}) plus the market value of outstanding debt (D_{it}) minus the replacement value of all remaining assets besides the capital stock (N_{it}) to the replacement value of the capital stock (K_{it}):[19]

$$Q_{it}^a = \frac{V_{it} + D_{it} - N_{it}}{K_{it}}$$

When using balance sheet data in the empirical analysis, no market values of equity and debt are available in the data source and they therefore have to be estimated.[20] The approach used in this paper is to estimate market values of equity based on a VAR-

16 Hayashi (1982), p. 214.

17 Beside the argument of data availability, the empirical results using stock market data have been rather disappointing, see e.g. the overview in Chirinko (1993).

18 See e.g. Erickson/Whited (2000a) p. 1034.

19 We include stocks of material as part of the capital stock, hence exclude it from N in the nominator.

20 See Perfect/Wiles (1994) discussing several alternative constructions of average Q.

forecasting model as was suggested by Abel and Blanchard (1986). Gilchrist and Himmelberg (1995, 1998) extended this approach to panel data.

The VAR-model we estimate contains three variables, pre-tax profits (*PTP*), sales (*S*) and cash flow (*CF*). The use of pre-tax profits instead of the theoretically more appealing after tax profits is inevitable because the apparent tax rate often shows implausible values and enormous variance. This is due to the fact that the database contains firms of different legal status, no information about the firms' dividend policy and firms carrying forward losses of former periods. In our final estimates we make use of the forecasts based on a VAR containing one lag, but we obtained comparable results when using two lags.

The equations of the VAR model using one lag can be written as

$$x_{1it} = d_{1i} + a_{11}x_{1i,t-1} + a_{12}x_{2i,t-1} + a_{13}x_{3i,t-1} + \varepsilon_{1it}$$

$$x_{2it} = d_{2i} + a_{21}x_{1i,t-1} + a_{22}x_{2i,t-1} + a_{23}x_{3i,t-1} + \varepsilon_{2it}$$

$$x_{3it} = d_{3i} + a_{31}x_{1i,t-1} + a_{32}x_{2i,t-1} + a_{33}x_{3i,t-1} + \varepsilon_{3it}$$

The equations of the VAR do not contain time dummies because we are interested in expected values conditioned on lagged values and fixed firm effects and not conditioned on specific time effects.[21]

As the usual LSDV estimator is known to be biased,[22] we apply a direct bias correction to estimate the dynamic equations containing fixed effects. All variables *j* are measured as deviations from their firm-individual means and therefore the equations do not contain firm-specific effects:

$$\widetilde{x}_{jit} = x_{jit} - \frac{1}{T}\sum_{t=1}^{T} x_{jit}$$

---

21 When time effects are included forecasts have to build upon special assumptions concerning the unknown future time effects.

22 See Nickell (1981).

Table 4.3: The Estimated Vector-Autoregressive Model for average Q, manufacturing

right-hand side variables	left-hand side variables: *PTP*	*CF*	*S*
PTP	0.852 (83.15)	0.137 (13.17)	1.549 (30.89)
CF	-0.008 (-2.1)	-0.015 (-4.03)	-0.158 (-8.97)
S	-0.005 (-2.78)	0.025 (14.22)	0.939 (109.15)

PTP Pre-Tax-Profits, *CF* Cash Flow, *S* Sales.

We find that pre-tax-profits and sales show a strong positive dependence on their lagged values, while the cash flow shows a minor negative partial correlation to its lagged value.

In the following we drop the tilde (the difference operator respectively) to ease readability.

In short notation the system of (seemingly) unrelated equations could be written as

$$\mathbf{x}_{it} = \mathbf{A}\mathbf{x}_{i,t-1} + \boldsymbol{\varepsilon}_{it}$$

Assuming a stationary process for each point of time t, the one-period-ahead forecast can be estimated by

$$\hat{\mathbf{x}}_{i,t+1} = E\left[\mathbf{x}_{i,t+1} \mid \mathbf{x}_{it}\right] = \hat{\mathbf{A}}\mathbf{x}_{i,t}$$

The two-period-ahead forecast can be estimated using the one-period-ahead forecast

$$\hat{\mathbf{x}}_{i,t+2} = E\left[\mathbf{x}_{i,t+2} \mid \mathbf{x}_{it}\right] = \hat{\mathbf{A}}\hat{\mathbf{x}}_{i,t+1}$$

and so on.[23]

Using these forecasts, the discounted value of future profits at time t can be calculated as follows, where it is assumed that profit is the first of the three variables used in the VAR[24]:

$$V_{i,t} = \sum_{\tau=1}^{\infty} E\left[x_{1i,t+\tau} \mid \mathbf{x}_{it}\right] \delta_{t,\tau}^{\tau}$$

$$\hat{V}_{i,t} = \sum_{\tau=1}^{\infty} \hat{x}_{1i,t+\tau}\, \delta_{t,\tau}^{\tau}$$

$$\text{with } \delta_{t,\tau}^{\tau} = \frac{1}{(1+r_{t,\tau})^{\tau}}.$$

We use the capital market interest rate (Umlaufsrendite festverzinslicher Wertpapiere inländischer Emittenten) as a measure of the opportunity costs to discount future profits. For each year the firm faces its forecasting problem, we use the actual term structure of capital market interest rates for 1 to 9 years maturity. For discounting even further forecasts the interest rate with a maturity of 9 years is used. In this respect we differ from earlier approaches (Gilchrist and Himmelberg 1995, 1998 and Bontempi et al. 2001), which for simplicity assume a fixed interest rate for all years and for all maturities.

Table 4.4 contains a comparison of estimated values of equity and balance sheet figures of equity for the three sectors manufacturing, construction and commerce.

---

23 This formulation of the forecast process does not take into account the existence of individual fixed effects. Either these effects have to be cancelled out by some data transformation (averaging or differencing) or they have to be estimated explicitly. See the Appendix for further details.

24 In our calculation we stop after 200 forecasting periods instead of using an indefinite forecast horizon.

Table 4.4: Balance sheet figures and estimates of equity

		n	$\overline{X}$	σ	*Median*	$Q_{75\%}$-$Q_{25\%}$
All	Balance sheet	23,140	41.95	398.72	2.48	10.20
	Estimated		119.29	961.77	7.88	36.10
Manufacturing	Balance sheet	13,420	62.71	517.93	4.49	16.92
	Estimated		183.69	1249.81	12.05	54.89
Construction	Balance sheet	1,120	43.45	211.94	2.16	8.94
	Estimated		45.41	235.90	3.63	26.99
Commerce	Balance sheet	8,600	9.36	40.04	1.15	3.59
	Estimated		28.44	169.68	5.06	18.47

We find that when comparing the means that the estimated market value of equity exceeds the book value by the factor of 2.9. Only for firms of the sector construction we find considerable less differences. The estimated market values exceed the book values only by 6%.

The estimated discounted value of future profits $\hat{V}_{i,t}$ is taken as part of the nominator to calculate firm and year-specific average Q:

$$Q_{it}^{a} = \frac{\hat{V}_{it} + D_{it} - N_{it}}{K_{it}}$$

4.3.4. Calculating marginal *Q*

So far we have estimated average Q^a using the estimated market value of equity.[25] To calculate marginal (fundamental) Q^m we follow a similar approach using the described Panel-VAR-technique. To calculate fundamental Q^m we first have to find a proxy for the marginal profitability of capital (MPK_{it}). Following Gilchrist and Himmelberg

25 From a theoretical point of view a marginal Q is more appropriate, see Gilchrist/Himmelberg (1998).

(1998) we use a measure based on a Cobb-Douglas-Production technology where capital is seen as a quasi-fixed factor of production:

$$Y = CK^{\alpha} L^{\beta} M^{\gamma}$$

with

Y	output
K	capital stock
L	labor
M	intermediates
α, β, γ	elasticities of production

Allowing for economies of scale

$$\alpha + \beta + \gamma = 1 + \lambda ,$$

the firm faces the following maximization problem:

$$\pi = YP - LW - MV - F$$

with

π profit
P output price
W wage
V price of intermediates
F fixed costs

subject to the Cobb-Douglas production function

$$\pi = AK^{\alpha} L^{\beta} M^{\gamma} P - LW - MV - F .$$

The marginal profitability of capital is given by

$$\frac{\partial \pi}{\partial K} = \frac{\partial \left(AK^{\alpha} L^{\beta} M^{\gamma} P - LW - MV - F \right)}{\partial K}$$

Allowing for non-perfect competition, the *MPK* can be written as

$$= \frac{\partial Y}{\partial K} P + \frac{\partial P}{\partial Y}\frac{\partial Y}{\partial K} Y = \frac{\partial Y}{\partial K} P + \frac{\partial P}{\partial Y}\frac{Y}{P} P \frac{\partial Y}{\partial K} = \frac{\partial Y}{\partial K} P + \eta^{-1} P \frac{\partial Y}{\partial K}$$

$$= \frac{\partial Y}{\partial K} P(1+\eta^{-1}) = \alpha K^{-1} Y P(1+\eta^{-1}) = \alpha(1+\eta^{-1})\frac{S}{K} = \theta \frac{S}{K}$$

with

η	price-elasticity of demand
S	sales

Therefore, the unknown *MPK* is proportional to the sales-to-capital-stock ratio. To estimate the unknown parameter θ we assume that on average the *MPK* equals the user costs of capital (U), which we measure as the sum of the apparent interest rate (r_i) and the rate of depreciation (d_i). Using the sectoral calculation of θ including all years and all firms belonging to sector j

$$\hat{\theta}_j = \frac{\overline{U_j}}{\overline{\left(\frac{S}{K}\right)_j}} = \sum_{i \in I(j)}^{N_j} \sum_{t=1}^{T} (r_i + d_i) \cdot \left[\sum_{i \in I(j)}^{N_j} \sum_{t=1}^{T} \left(\frac{S}{K}\right)_{it} \right]^{-1}$$

the firm and year-specific marginal profitability of capital is estimated as

$$\hat{MPK}_{it} \approx \hat{\theta}_j \left(\frac{S}{K}\right)_{it}$$

Q^m is then calculated as the present value of estimated future marginal profitabilities of capital

$$Q_{i,t}^m = \sum_{\tau=1}^{\infty} E(MPK_{it}) \delta_{i,t,\tau}^{\tau} \approx \hat{\theta}_j \sum_{\tau=1}^{\infty} \left(\frac{S}{K}\right)_{i,t+\tau} \delta_{i,t,\tau}^{\tau}$$

$$\text{with } \delta_{i,t,\tau}^{\tau} = \frac{(1+d_i)^{\tau}}{(1+r_{t,\tau})^{\tau}}$$

where the market interest rate for the relevant maturity and firm specific depreciation rates are used.[26] The estimated VAR model with one lag includes the estimated *MPK*, the cash flow (*CF*) and the operating income (*OI*), both measured as the ratio to the capital stock.

Table 4.5: The Estimated Vector-Autoregressive Model for marginal Q, manufacturing

right-hand side variables	left-hand side variables: *MPK*	*CFK*	*OIK*
MPK	0.901 (132.09)	0.481 (9.34)	-0.068 (-2.28)
CFK	-0.003 (-7.76)	-0.012 (-3.82)	-0.015 (-8.53)
OIK	-0.036 (-17.21)	0.212 (13.64)	0.698 (77.24)

MPK Marginal Profitability of Capital, *CFK* Cash Flow divided by the adjusted capital stock, *OIK* Operational Income divided by the adjusted capital stock.

It is evident that marginal profitability of capital as well as operational income exhibits much stronger dependence on their lagged value. The explanatory power of the VAR for cash flow is significantly smaller.

4.3.5. Empirical Results

The following table contains some descriptive statistics for the estimated average *Q* and marginal *Q*. From the table as well as from the graph containing kernel-density estimations for the two *Q*-measures, it can be seen that average *Q* exhibits a higher level

---

26 While Gilchrist and Himmelberg (1995) assume a constant value for all firms and all years we take the individual depreciation rates, resulting mainly from different ratios of structure to equipment for individual firms, as well as the interest term strucuture into account.

and greater variance.[27] While the average Q is somewhat higher than the expected equilibrium value, the estimated marginal Q is in average slightly too low.

We find that the mean of the average Q is 2.5 times the mean of the calculated marginal Q. While the marginal Q is roughly equal in the three sectors manufacturing, construction and commerce we find a considerable lower value for average Q when looking at construction firms only. Both measures of Q deviate in average from the expected equilibrium value of 1, average Q is above, marginal Q is below that value.

Table 4.6: Descriptive statistics of the estimated Qs

		n	$\overline{X}$	σ	*Median*	$Q_{75\%}$-$Q_{25\%}$
All	Average Q	23,140	1.59	1.81	1.09	1.62
	Marginal Q		0.64	0.47	0.51	0.44
Manufacturing	Average Q	13,420	1.52	1.76	1.04	1.51
	Marginal Q		0.65	0.45	0.53	0.41
Construction	Average Q	1,120	1.20	1.94	0.76	1.54
	Marginal Q		0.63	0.37	0.55	0.41
Commerce	Average Q	8,600	1.76	1.86	1.24	1.80
	Marginal Q		0.62	0.51	0.47	0.49

The following kernel density estimation displays the distribution of the calculated marginal and average Q-measures. While the distribution of both measures display a considerable skewness, the dispersion of average Q exceeds the dispersion of marginal Q considerably.

27 To control for outliers we drop the upper and lower 0.5% quantils for both (average and marginal) Q-measures.

Fig. 4.7: Kernel-density estimations for the estimated Qs all sectors

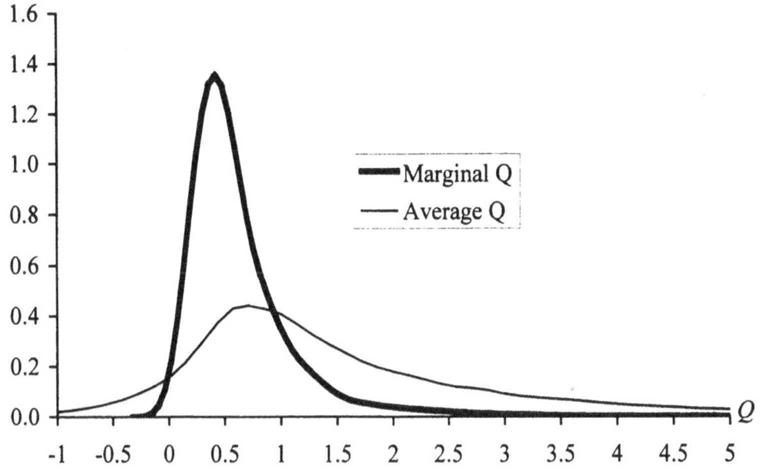

Note: The kernel used was triangular with a bandwidth of 0.25.

Fig. 4.8: Kernel-density estimations for the estimated average Qs in three sectors

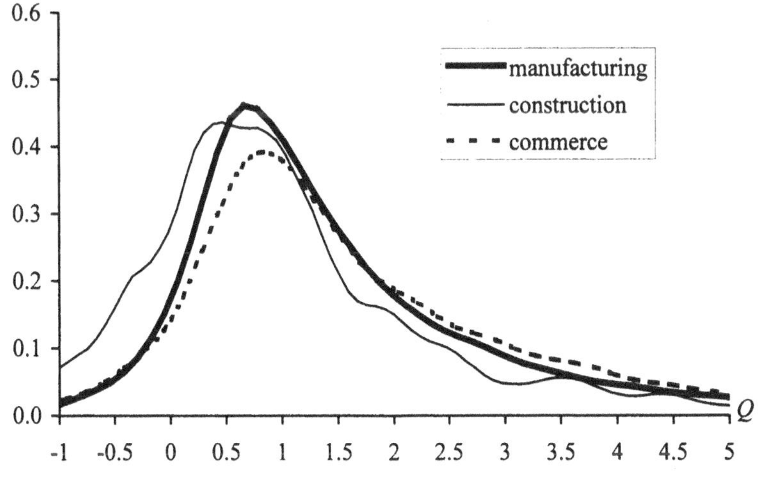

Note: The kernel used was triangular with a bandwidth of 0.4.

When comparing the distributions of average Q in the three main sectors, we find that the distributions are skewed and that the highest densities are just below 1. The distribution for the sector construction is shifted somewhat to the left.

Fig. 4.9: Kernel-density estimations for the estimated marginal Qs in three sectors

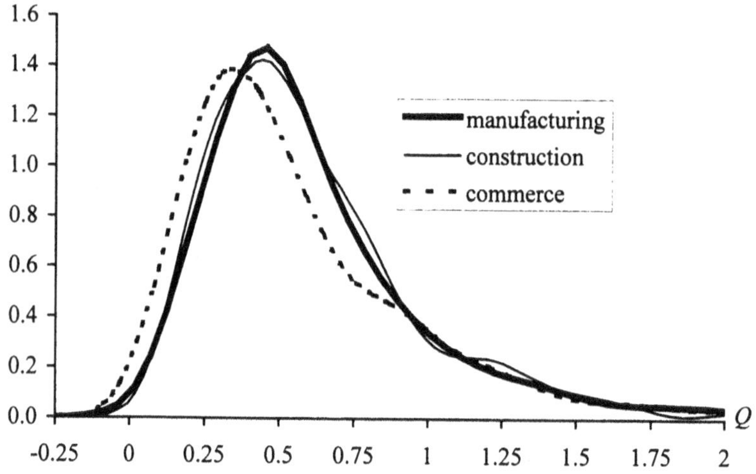

Note: The kernel used was triangular with a bandwidth of 0.2.

The distributions for marginal Q in the three sectors resemble and we find that especially the distribution for manufacturing and construction are very close, the distribution for commerce has similar shape but lower mean.

4.4. Conclusion

In this chapter we discussed the measurement problems when making use of firm level balance sheet data to estimate Q-investment functions. The problems we see as most serious for the measurement of the capital stock at replacement values as well as the measurement of Q.

For calculating the capital stock we developed an approach based on the idea of the perpetual inventory method. The main feature is the disaggregation of the capital stock into equipment and structures and into different vintages. The calculation is based on sectoral depreciation data because we assume the balance sheet figures not to be adequate.

When calculating Q two different approaches were followed, both based on the direct forecasting via a vector autoregressive model for panel data. While the measure of average Q relies on forecasted future profits to calculate market values of equity, the marginal Q measure is based on forecasted marginal profitabilities of capital.

To assess the relation between the Q measures and investment we followed a non-parametric approach, which is most flexible and facilitates a condensed description of the information contained in the data. For both Q measures the non-parametric results hint for a fairly linear bivariate relation to the investment ratio.

5. Empirical findings

This chapter contains the empirical results of the investment analysis. The investment functions are estimated using a bias-corrected estimator to take into account the resulting bias when using the lagged endogenous variable.[1] We prefer the direct bias correction method compared to instrumentation for two reasons. First, when analyzing different estimators, simulation studies (Kiviet (1995), Judson and Owen (1999), Hansen (2001)) find a corrected LSDV estimator superior compared to GMM-estimators. This result was confirmed in the detailed analysis of dynamic panel data estimation techniques of chapter 3.

Second, as is usually the case when using large micro data files containing mainly cross-section information, the correlations of the variables of interest are rather low in almost all respects. Therefore, the use of differences instead of levels considerably reduces the amount of information contained in the data used for estimation. Instrumental estimation is known to be problematic when instruments are rather weak.[2] When instruments are weak, the results are extremely sensitive to the choice of instruments, leading to a large number of degrees of freedom for the researcher. We therefore regard it as an advantage of the bias correction approach that it restricts these facilities.[3]

Before turning to the estimated investment functions we present some descriptive statistics. One fact that should be taken into account when interpreting the regression results is, that investment is measured as the ratio to the beginning of period capital stock.[4] Because the beginning of period capital stock can be very small compared to the investment taking place, very large ratios can result.[5] This leads to the somewhat surprising finding that the mean of the investment ratio for equipment and the

---

1 See chapter 3 for details about the estimation procedure.

2 When instrumenting the difference of Q by the lagged difference of Q we loose about 99% of the information contained in the difference of Q!

3 A comparison of the results using GMM-methods is given in chapter 4.

4 The time-to-build in our view supports the use of beginning of period values as regressors. See Zhou (2000).

5 The most extreme values of the all variables inclueded in the analysis were removed by dropping the highest and lowest 0.5% quantiles prior to the analysis. See chapter 5 for details.

investment ratio for structures exceed the investment ratio for aggregate investment. We observe too, that the mean of the investment ratios is by far larger than the ratio of the sum of investment to the sum of the beginning of period capital stock. The next table displays these facts.

Especially for structures, where one would expect rather low investment ratios due to the long lifetime of these capital goods, we find a mean of investment ratios about four times the ratio of all investment in structures to the sum of all structures. For equipment and aggregate investment the difference is less pronounced.

Table 5.1: Descriptive statistics for class sizes

	I/K	I^e/K^e	I^s/K^s
mean of ratios	0.145	0.237	0.200
ratio of sums*	0.119	0.173	0.051

* weighted mean

5.1. Nonparametric regression results

Before estimating parametrically the dynamic investment equations using the two different measures of Q we take a non-parametric approach to see whether we can find any indication of a linear relation in the bivariate case. We estimate three non-parametric regressions explaining the investment ratio by its lagged value, average and marginal Q respectively. When examining the kernel regressions it has to be kept in mind that this bivariate analysis does not necessarily coincide with the partial influence displayed in multivariate analysis. Nevertheless the nonparametric regressions can through their flexibility hint for relations that might be concealed in parametric linear regressions.

5.1.1. Aggregate investment

Fig. 5.1 and Fig. 5.2 contain the nonparametric regression as well as the distribution of the explanatory variable. The regression curve is reliable only if the density of the explanatory variable is not too low, which might lead to unreliable estimates caused by few irregular values.

Fig. 5.1: Kernel regression for aggregate investment: $I/K = f(I_{-1}/K_{-1})$

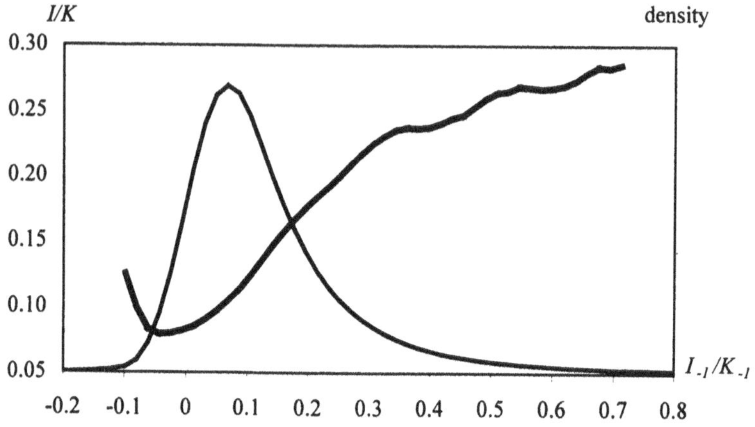

Note: Triangular kernel, bandwith = 0.1.

The bivariate regression between aggregate investment and it´s lagged value displays a linear positive relationship over almost the complete range of lagged investment values. Only for the few lowest lagged investment ratios the relation is negative.

Fig. 5.2: Kernel regression for aggregate investment: $I/K = f(Q^a)$

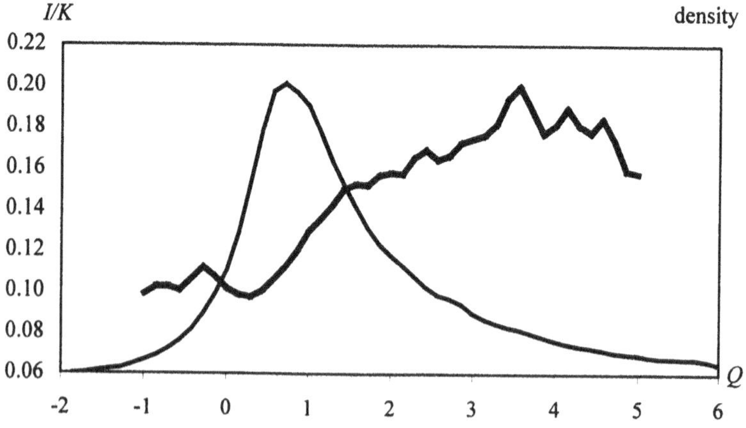

Note: Triangular kernel, bandwidth = 0.25.

Fig. 5.3: Kernel regression for aggregate investment: $I/K = f(Q^m)$

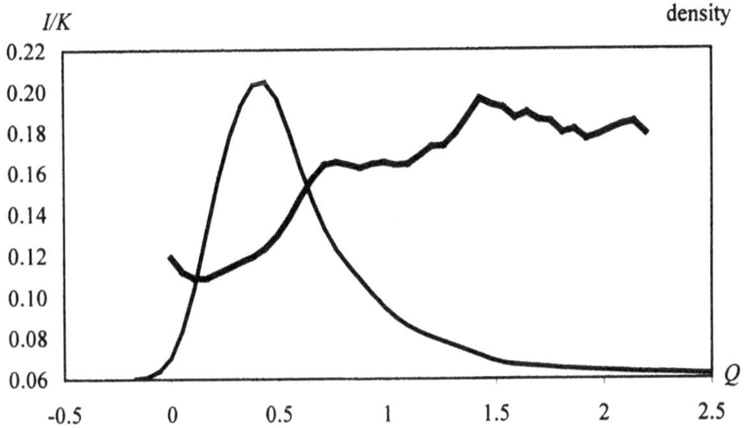

Note: Triangular kernel, bandwidth = 0.15.

The nonparametric regression between average Q and aggregate investment hints for a linear bivariate relationship as well. Only at the tails of the Q^a-distribution we find deviations from the linear positive relation. The finding for marginal Q is similar and hints in the relevant range for a near linear relationship, too.

5.1.2. Disaggregate investment

5.1.2.1. Equipment

Because aggregate investment consists of investment in equipment as well as investment in structures, we perform the same analysis at the disaggregate level. Because of the strong differences in lifetimes, we find very different investment ratios for equipment compared to structures.

Fig. 5.4: Kernel regression: lagged and current investment in equipment: $I^e/K^e = f(I^e_{-1}/K^e_{-1})$

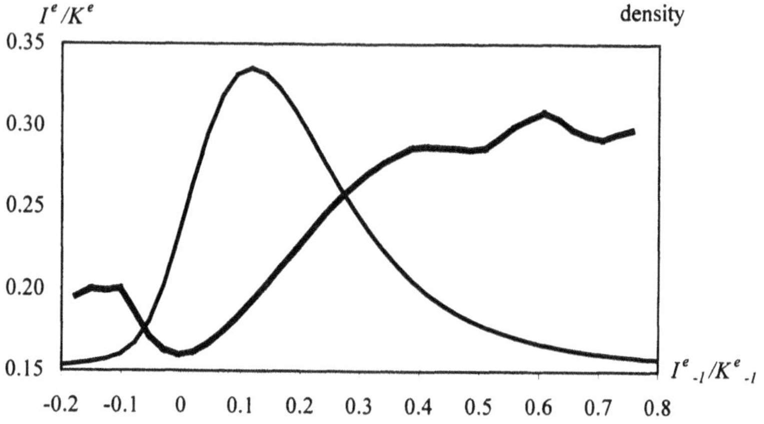

Note: Triangular kernel, bandwidth = 0.1.

The diagram displays the relation between investment and lagged investment in equipment. We find a positive linear relation for positive lagged investment in equipment, while for negative investment ratios of lagged investment we find a downward sloping curve.

The relation between average Q and investment in equipment is somewhat irregular, but over the relevant range where the mass of the Q^a-distribution is concentrated, we find a positive relation that could be roughly approximated by a linear regression line.[6]

---

6 For an attempt to model nonlinear response of firm investment on Q see Barnett/Sakellaris (1998).

Fig. 5.5: Kernel regression: Average Q and investment in equipment: $I^e/K^e = f(Q^a)$

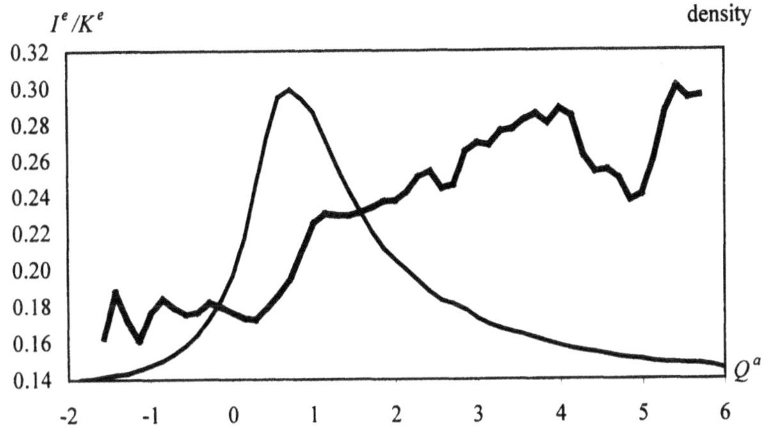

Note: Triangular kernel, bandwidth = 0.25.

For marginal Q the relation to investment in equipment is almost linear over the relevant range. Only for the few highest marginal Q values, we find a downward sloping relation.

Fig. 5.6: Kernel regression: Marginal Q and investment in equipment: $I^e/K^e = f(Q^m)$

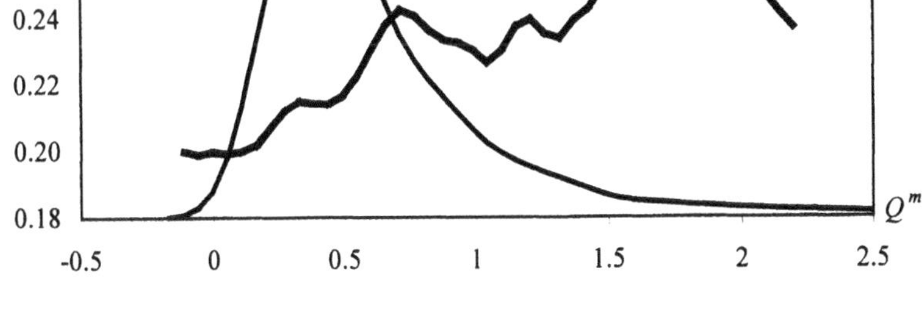

Note: Triangular kernel, bandwidth = 0.15.

5.1.2.2. Structures

The nonparametric regression between investment in structures and the lagged value thereof reveals a very irregular relation. Over the range of lagged investment ratios where the mass of the distribution is concentrated, the relation is fairly linear and downward sloping. This finding strengthens the argument for a disaggregate analysis. Because the relation between investment and lagged investment is in an opposite manner for equipment and structures. The aggregation would conceal such differences.

Fig. 5.7: Kernel regression: lagged and current investment in structures:
$I^s/K^s = f(I^s_{-1}/K^s_{-1})$

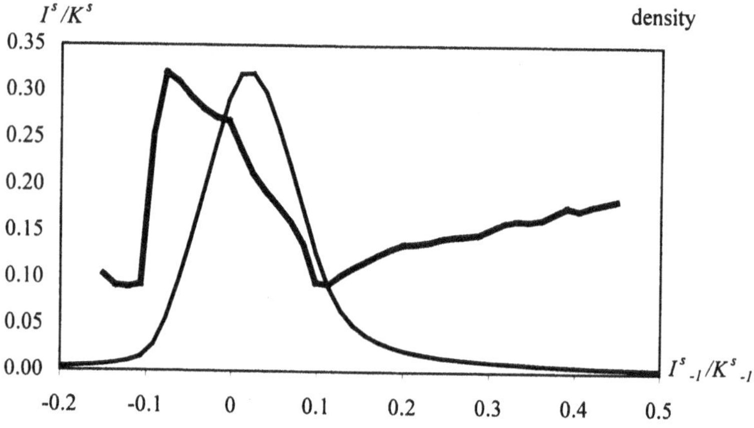

Note: Triangular kernel, bandwidth = 0.1.

There is only a very irregular relation between average Q and investment in structures present. For the range around the equilibrium value slightly positive relation could be seen, but the relation is covered by the irregularities.

Fig. 5.8: Kernel regression: Average Q and investment in structures: $I^s/K^s = f(Q^a)$

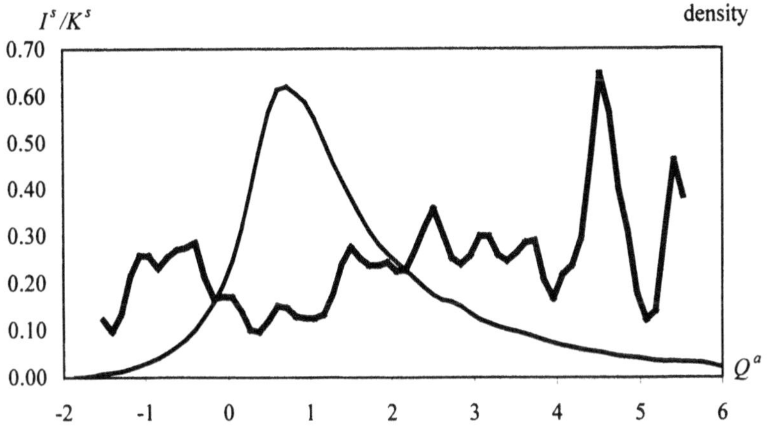

Note: Triangular kernel, bandwidth = 0.25.

The overall relation between marginal Q and investment in structures is positive, but the slope is small and for below average Q-values the relation is negative.

Fig. 5.9: Kernel regression: Marginal Q and investment in structures: $I^s/K^s = f(Q^m)$

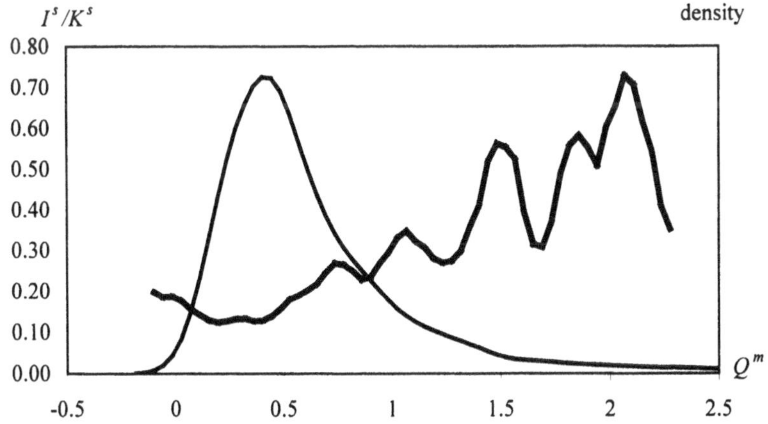

Note: Triangular kernel, bandwidth = 0.15.

To conclude the nonparametric regression approach, we can state that the relations between the explanatory variables under consideration, lagged investment, average and marginal Q and the investment ratio differ considerably between investment in equipment and investment in structures. While equipment is roughly linear positive related to the three explanatory variables, the relation to investment in structures is very irregular.

5.2. Aggregate and disaggregate Q-investment functions

The nonparametric analysis of chapter 5.1. revealed that the investment ratios as well as the relation to the lagged investment ratio and to the Q-measures differed considerably for structures and equipment. Hence we estimate Q-investment functions for investment disaggregated into equipment and structures as well.

5.2.1. Aggregate investment

We first estimate a dynamic Q-investment function for all firms belonging to very different sectors, broadly classified into manufacturing, construction and commerce.[7]

Average Q:

$$\widehat{\left(\frac{I}{K}\right)} = a_i + \underset{(17.43)}{0.114}\left(\frac{I}{K}\right)_{-1} + \underset{(35.85)}{0.061}\, Q^a_{-1} \qquad n = 23{,}140$$

Turning to average Q first, we find that the investment ratio depends positively and highly significant on Q^a as well as on the lagged investment ratio.

Marginal Q:

$$\widehat{\left(\frac{I}{K}\right)} = a_i + \underset{(6.76)}{0.048}\left(\frac{I}{K}\right)_{-1} + \underset{(26.85)}{0.264}\, Q^m_{-1} \qquad n = 23{,}140$$

We find both measures of Q as well as the lagged investment ratio to be highly significant.[8] In both equations the lagged investment ratio is highly significant as well.

---

7 See chapter 5.1. for further details.

According to the t-values, the investment ratio correlates partially considerable stronger with average Q compared to the lagged investment ratio. Comparing the parameters for the two Q-measures, we find that the parameter of marginal Q is about four times the parameter of average Q. But it has to be taken into account that average Q has a standard deviation almost four times the standard deviation of marginal Q. The parameter of average Q is at the upper bound of the interval of parameters found in empirical studies using stock market data rather than the direct forecasting approach.[9] The higher parameter of marginal Q is closer to the theoretical expectations about its value when trying to interpret the regression parameter as the capital stock adjustment cost parameter. However, because of the dependence of the parameter value on the standard deviation of the Q measure, the parameter should be interpreted with care. Whited (1994) discusses the problems of inferring adjustment cost parameters from the Q-parameter in detail.

Even if the simple variance decomposition does not hold exactly in the context of the dynamic panel data estimation, the share of explained variance is still a useful indicator of the explanatory power of the estimated equation. It turns out that average Q (5%) explains a slightly larger part of investment compared to marginal Q (4%).

As marginal and average Q were measured quite differently, one might ask whether the information is rather redundant, or whether the two measures are independent of one another. As shown by Hayashi (1982), theoretically the two measures can be interchanged only in the case of perfect competition and linear homogeneous technology.

Therefore, comparing the two different measures can also be seen as an indirect test of the combined hypothesis of the production function and the adjustment cost function of the capital stock being linearly homogeneous and of perfect competition. Of course, the comparison is based on the operationalisation of both concepts and therefore depends strongly on the adequacy of the operationalisation procedure. For the estimated dynamic investment function containing marginal as well as average Q we find.

---

8 These results confirm the significant influence of Q^a on German firms investment spending found when using sectoral data, see Behr/Bellgardt (1998, 2000). For results for German firms using stock market data see Audretsch/Elston (2002).

9 See e.g. Whited (1992).

$$\widehat{\left(\frac{I}{K}\right)} = a_i + \underset{(6.98)}{0.048}\left(\frac{I}{K}\right)_{-1} + \underset{(34.74)}{0.058}\, Q^a_{-1} + \underset{(25.34)}{0.243}\, Q^m_{-1} \quad n = 23{,}140$$

Both measures of Q contain valuable and largely independent information explaining the investment behavior of firms. According to the t-values, average Q does explain partially a somewhat larger amount of the investment compared to marginal Q. Together both measures of investment profitability explain about 10% of the variation of investment according to the naive measure of residual sum of squares divided by total sum of squares. The finding of fairly independent information in the two different measures of Q casts doubt on the theoretical assumptions of perfect competition and linear homogenous technology, which would make the use of the two measures interchangeable.

5.2.2. Equipment

The estimated dynamic function for investment in equipment shows that investment in equipment is less dependent on its lagged value compared to aggregate investment. This result is evident for the average as well as for the marginal Q-investment function. In both equations the influence of the Q-variable is almost identically.

Average Q:

$$\widehat{\left(\frac{I}{K}\right)} = a_i + \underset{(5.47)}{0.035}\left(\frac{I}{K}\right)_{-1} + \underset{(26.11)}{0.067}\, Q^a_{-1} \quad n = 23{,}140$$

Marginal Q:

$$\widehat{\left(\frac{I}{K}\right)} = a_i + \underset{(2.00)}{0.013}\left(\frac{I}{K}\right)_{-1} + \underset{(17.30)}{0.250}\, Q^m_{-1} \quad n = 23{,}140$$

When using both Q-measures simultaneously, we get the corresponding results. The dependence on lagged investment is considerably lower compared to aggregate investment, but the parameters for the Q-measures remain similar.

$$\widehat{\left(\frac{I}{K}\right)} = a_i + \underset{(1.11)}{0.007}\left(\frac{I}{K}\right)_{-1} + \underset{(25.32)}{0.064}\, Q^a_{-1} + \underset{(16.10)}{0.230}\, Q^m_{-1} \quad n = 23{,}140$$

5.2.3. Structures

For investment in structures the nonparametric analysis revealed only a very weak dependence of the investment ratio and its lagged value. The bivariate correlation between the investment ratio and the Q-measures appeared to be modestly. These finding is confirmed in the parametric analysis. In both regression equations for structures we find no significant dependence of the investment ratio on its lagged value. While both Q-measures appear statistically significant, the standard deviations of the parameters are considerably larger compared to the investment equations for equipment.

Average Q:

$$\widehat{\left(\frac{I}{K}\right)} = a_i + \underset{(0.83)}{0.006}\left(\frac{I}{K}\right)_{-1} + \underset{(4.98)}{0.096}\, Q^a_{-1} \qquad n = 23{,}140$$

Marginal Q:

$$\widehat{\left(\frac{I}{K}\right)} = a_i + \underset{(0.29)}{0.002}\left(\frac{I}{K}\right)_{-1} + \underset{(8.03)}{0.847}\, Q^m_{-1} \qquad n = 23{,}140$$

When considering both Q-measures, we find again that the partial influences remain unchanged:

$$\widehat{\left(\frac{I}{K}\right)} = a_i + \underset{(0.37)}{0.003}\left(\frac{I}{K}\right)_{-1} + \underset{(4.45)}{0.086}\, Q^a_{-1} + \underset{(7.71)}{0.815}\, Q^m_{-1} \qquad n = 23{,}140$$

5.2.4. Results for classes of firm size

In this section we analyze the investment behavior of three classes of firm size. The following table contains descriptive measures for these three classes of firm size.[10]

---

10 The variable used to classify firms according to size is total assets (TA, balance sheet total) in 1988, the year prior to the estimation period. Because only the balance sheet total is observable for lenders and outsiders, we do not correct the balance sheet total for the capital stock at replacement values. The grouping according to the balance sheet total corrected for the revaluation of the capital stock leads to no major changes in the results.

As can be seen, the investment ratio decreases with firm size from 16.5 % in the smallest class of firms to only 12.8 % in the class containing the largest firms. While marginal Q also decreases from 0.68 for the smallest firms to only 0.62 in the class of the largest firms, there is no such evidence for average Q.

Table 5.2: Descriptive statistics for class sizes

Averages, standard deviation in parentheses

	All	*class 1 (smallest)*	*class 2*	*class 3 (largest)*
n	2,3140	7,720	7,710	7,710
I/K	0.145	0.165	0.143	0.128
	(0.18)	(0.22)	(0.17)	(0.13)
I^e/K^e	0.237	0.263	0.236	0.211
	(0.26)	(0.31)	(0.25)	(0.2)
I^s/K^s	0.2	0.307	0.181	0.112
	(1.73)	(2.34)	(1.55)	(1.04)
Q^m	1.592	1.792	1.518	1.465
	(1.81)	(1.91)	(1.71)	(1.77)
Q^a	0.636	0.683	0.606	0.617
	(0.47)	(0.52)	(0.43)	(0.44)
TA	1.592	1.792	1.518	1.465
	(1.81)	(1.91)	(1.71)	(1.77)

Next we estimate dynamic investment functions for the three different size-classes using a direct bias correction estimation method. Table 5.3 contains the results. It can be seen that the firms belonging to different classes exhibit strong differences in their investment behavior. The influence of the lagged investment ratio increases from 0.114 for the class of smallest to 0.213 for the class of largest firms and is significantly different from 0 in all classes. Of course, it has to be borne in mind that the smaller the capital stocks the less continuous will the investment process of a firm be according to pure aggregation effects. For larger firms the aggregation will smooth out such discontinuities. The parameter for average Q almost halves from 0.075 for the smallest firms to only 0.038 for the largest firms. Therefore it can be stated that the larger the firms the more its investment ratio is influenced by its past investment behavior and the less by the profitability, measured through average Q, into account.

For investment in equipment we find also a decreasing influence of Q^a for larger firms, albeit less pronounced compared to aggregate investment. Lagged investment is not significant for the smallest of firms. Again we find an increasing effect of lagged investment for larger firm.

In no class we find the investment in structures to depend on lagged investment. While average Q is significant in all classes the influence is strongest for mid sized firms.

Table 5.3: Average Q investment functions for class sizes

		All	*class 1 (smallest)*	*class 2*	*class 3 (largest)*
	n	2,3140	7,720	7,710	7,710
Aggregate	$(I/K)_{i,t-1}$	0.1144	0.0659	0.1389	0.2127
		(17.43)	(5.85)	(12.04)	(19.09)
	$Q^a_{i,t-1}$	0.0606	0.0753	0.0613	0.0384
		(35.85)	(23.48)	(19.82)	(17.48)
Equipment	$(I/K)_{i,t-1}$	0.0354	-0.0041	0.059	0.1043
		(5.47)	(-0.37)	(5.17)	(9.13)
	$Q^a_{i,t-1}$	0.0669	0.0767	0.0675	0.0517
		(26.11)	(16.00)	(14.73)	(14.09)
Structures	$(I/K)_{i,t-1}$	0.0058	0.0053	0.0017	0.0202
		(0.83)	(0.44)	(0.14)	(1.66)
	$Q^a_{i,t-1}$	0.0964	0.1163	0.1278	0.0292
		(6.51)	(2.86)	(6.47)	(1.90)

When using marginal Q the findings for the different size classes are similar concerning the increasing influence of lagged investment for increasing firm size. For marginal Q

there is less evidence of decreasing influence with firm size compared to average *Q*. Each of the three different size classes shows a strong and significant reaction to marginal *Q*. In opposite to the results for average *Q* there is no decrease in the *Q*-dependence apparent.

While investment in equipment of the largest firms reacts most strongly on marginal *Q*, like it was the case for average *Q* as well, mid sized firms react strongest on marginal *Q* when investing in structures.

Table 5.4: Marginal Q investment functions for class sizes

		All	*class 1 (smallest)*	*class 2*	*class 3 (largest)*
	n	23,140	7,720	7,710	7,710
Aggregate	$(I/K)_{i,t-1}$	0.0473	0.0033	0.0649	0.1476
		(6.76)	(0.27)	(5.30)	(12.61)
	$Q^m_{i,t-1}$	0.2639	0.261	0.2843	0.2417
		(26.85)	(15.01)	(16.49)	(15.36)
Equipment	$(I/K)_{i,t-1}$	0.0134	-0.021	0.0354	0.071
		(2.00)	(-1.84)	(3.00)	(6.01)
	$Q^m_{i,t-1}$	0.2503	0.2221	0.26	0.3085
		(17.30)	(8.89)	(10.47)	(11.93)
Structures	$(I/K)_{i,t-1}$	0.002	0.0009	-0.0047	0.0203
		(0.29)	(0.07)	(-0.39)	(1.67)
	$Q^m_{i,t-1}$	0.8475	1.0675	0.8311	0.2419
		(8.03)	(5.22)	(5.01)	(1.62)

5.2.5. Results for three main sectors

The database used throughout this work consists of 2,314 firms belonging to different sectors. Considering three broad sectors, we have 1,342 manufacturing firms, 112 firms belonging to the sector construction and 8,600 firms belonging to the sector commerce.

When comparing the descriptive results for these sectors, we find that firms of the sector commerce have in average Q values considerable higher compared to manufacturing firms. Construction firms have by far the lowest average Q values. When comparing marginal Q averages, we find only minor differences between the sectors.

Table 5.5: Descriptive Statistics

(mean, standard deviation in parentheses)

	All	*Manufact.*	*Construct.*	*Commerce*
n	23,140	13,420	1,120	8,600
I/K	0.145	0.141	0.171	0.149
	(0.18)	(0.16)	(0.18)	(0.2)
Q^a	1.592	1.517	1.201	1.76
	(1.81)	(1.76)	(1.94)	(1.86)
Q^m	0.636	0.649	0.633	0.616
	(0.47)	(0.45)	(0.37)	(0.51)

The descriptive results for these sectors reveal too, that firms of the sector commerce have in average Q values considerable higher compared to manufacturing firms. Construction firms have by far the lowest average Q values. When comparing marginal Q averages, we find only minor differences between the sectors.

The estimated investment functions including average Q reveal differences mainly in the parameter of lagged investment. The investment of construction firms depends strongest on lagged investment, while the commerce firms exhibit the lowest parameter. For average Q we find that manufacturing firms react stronger compared to commerce firms. The difference in the parameter is about 13%.

Table 5.6: Average Q investment functions for sectors

(parameter, t-value in parentheses)

	All	*Manufact.*	*Construct.*	*Commerce*
n	23,140	13,420	1,120	8,600
$(I/K)_{i,t-1}$	0.1144	0.1363	0.181	0.0841
	(17.43)	(15.97)	(6.18)	(7.72)
$Q^a_{i,t-1}$	0.0606	0.0640	0.0546	0.0566
	(35.85)	(29.99)	(8.31)	(19.08)

While we find a similar result for lagged investment, when using marginal Q as a regressor, the results for Q differ. In opposite to the findings for average Q the manufacturing firms react less then firms belonging to the sector commerce and the sector construction on changes in the measure of profitability.

Table 5.7: Marginal Q investment functions for sectors

(parameter, t-value in parentheses)

	All	*Manufact.*	*Construct.*	*Commerce*
n	23,140	13,420	1,120	8,600
$(I/K)_{i,t-1}$	0.0473	0.0688	0.0916	0.0142
	(6.76)	(7.47)	(2.97)	(1.24)
$Q^m_{i,t-1}$	0.2639	0.2182	0.5015	0.3404
	(26.85)	(20.11)	(6.76)	(17.05)

To conclude, we can state that a very strong influence of the Q-measures was found in all of the three broad sectors considered. The two different Q-measures, we already found to be partially only weakly correlated, both have strong and significant explanatory power for investment. In all sectors investment is positively related to lagged investment hinting for gradual adjustments to the optimal capital stock.

5.3. Testing for liqudity effects in three sectors: manufacturing, construction, commerce

Because the investment behavior of manufacturing firms is expected to differ from the investment behavior of construction and commerce firms, these sectors are in the following analyzed separately.

5.3.1. Liquidity effects in manufacturing firms investment behavior

In this section we study the effects of liquidity on manufacturing firms investment decisions in depth.

The following dynamic investment equation is estimated using a direct bias correction method[11] and contains beside average Q sales (S) as well as the cash flow (CF).[12]

Q-investment function for aggregate investment

$$\widehat{\left(\frac{I}{K}\right)_t} = a_i + \underset{(8.30)}{0.0738}\left(\frac{I}{K}\right)_{t-1} + \underset{(26.62)}{0.0568}\, Q_{t-1}^{a} + \underset{(17.65)}{0.0180}\left(\frac{S}{K}\right)_{t-1} - \underset{(-0.20)}{0.0003}\left(\frac{CF}{K}\right)_{t-1}$$

$$n = 13{,}420$$

The cash flow parameter appears insignificant but the sales variable indicates that there is still some relevant information in sales not captured by the measure of Q. But by far the measure of profitability (Q^a) is more powerful in explaining investment behavior compared to sales and cash flow. We interpret the result therefore as supporting evidence for the Q theory of investment. The results do not hint for the presence of a significant independent cash flow influence.[13]

It is well known that investment in equipment and structures follows very different patterns. Therefore we estimate in the next step investment functions separately for equipment and structures. While there are attempts to split the firm's total profits into

---

11 See chapter 4 for details. In all estimated investment functions time dummies are included.

12 The comparable LSDV and GMM estimates are contained in the appendix.

13 In the context of a user cost model including several lags, von Kalckreuth found a significant cash flow influence indicating the existence of liquidity constraints for German firms. See von Kalckreuth (2001).

profits caused by equipment and profits caused by structures we see such attempts as overoptimistic. Because neither sales nor profits are "earmarked" solely dividing variables by the capital stock of equipment or structures does not seem very promising.[14] Therefore in both investment equations we use the Q-variable based on expected profits of the firm as a regressor.

Q-investment function for investment in equipment

$$\left(\frac{\hat{I}^e}{K^e}\right)_t = a_i + \underset{(5.04)}{0.0434}\left(\frac{I^e}{K^e}\right)_{t-1} + \underset{(20.92)}{0.0656}\, Q^a_{t-1} + \underset{(13.25)}{0.0194}\left(\frac{S}{K}\right)_{t-1} - \underset{(-0.75)}{0.0018}\left(\frac{CF}{K}\right)_{t-1}$$

$n = 13{,}420$

Q-investment function for investment in structures

$$\left(\frac{\hat{I}^s}{K^s}\right)_t = a_i + \underset{(0.59)}{0.0056}\left(\frac{I^e}{K^e}\right)_{t-1} + \underset{(3.30)}{0.0888}\, Q^a_{t-1} + \underset{(3.61)}{0.0437}\left(\frac{S}{K}\right)_{t-1} + \underset{(0.50)}{0.0103}\left(\frac{CF}{K}\right)_{t-1}$$

$n = 13{,}420$

Again Q has the strongest explanatory power for investment in equipment, while about the same low explanatory power for investment in structures as the sales variable.[15] While lagged investment influences significantly investment in equipment, the investment in structures does not depend significantly on last year's investment. Both types of investment increase with sales, while no evidence is found for a significant cash flow dependence on investment.[16]

---

14 But see Bontempi (2001) et. al. for such an attempt and empirical results. A theoretical treatment is given in Wildasin (1984).

15 See Cuthbertson/Gasparro (1995) for evidence for manufacturing in the UK for a stock market based Q.

16 This observation is consistent with the neoclassical reasoning that cash flow should not increase investment when investment opportunities are held constant. It is hoped that the measurement of Q extracts the informatin contained in cash flow concerning investment opportunities. While cash flow is often found to effect investment significantly, Blanchard / Lopez-de-Silanes and Shleifer (1994) find no effect of cash windfalls on investment when analysing U.S. firms in the context of the Q-theory.

5.3.1.1. Results for classes of firm size

In this section we investigate the investment behavior of German firms taking into account the firm size. Especially we want to analyze the differences in firm's investment behavior when the firms are grouped a priori into three different classes of firm size.

The following table contains descriptive measures for three classes of firm size. The variable used to classify firms according to size is total assets (*TA*, balance sheet total assets) in 1988, the year prior to the estimation period.[17]

As can be seen, the investment ratio is decreasing in firm size from 16.2 % in the smallest class of firms to only 12.2 % in the two classes containing the largest firms. There is no such evidence for average *Q*, which is in average quite similar in the different classes. The average ratio of cash flow to capital stock is increasing with firm size and averages about the value of 0.155. The ratio of sales to capital stock shows the opposite effect. Comparing the smallest class with a ratio of about 4.3 with the ratio (2.9) for the largest firms we find a considerable larger sales productivity of the capital stock for smaller firms.

---

17 Because only the balance sheet total is observable for lenders and outsiders, we do not correct the balance sheet total for the capital stock at replacement values. The grouping according to the balance sheet total corrected for the revaluation of the capital stock leads to no major changes in the results.

Table 5.8: Descriptive Statistics, Averages, standard deviation in parentheses

	All	*class 1 (smallest)*	*class 2*	*class 3 (largest)*
n	13420	4480	4470	4470
I/K	0.141	0.162	0.137	0.122
	(0.16)	(0.2)	(0.15)	(0.11)
I^e/K^e	0.203	0.223	0.203	0.183
	(0.23)	(0.28)	(0.22)	(0.16)
I^s/K^s	0.182	0.299	0.161	0.086
	(1.6)	(2.29)	(1.47)	(0.46)
Q^a	1.517	1.668	1.454	1.429
	(1.76)	(1.87)	(1.7)	(1.69)
S/K	3.509	4.296	3.334	2.895
	(3.57)	(5.09)	(2.68)	(2.03)
CF/K	0.155	0.123	0.143	0.197
	(0.77)	(1.05)	(0.73)	(0.37)
RTA	175.348	6.165	22.626	497.632
	(1232.03)	(4.95)	(12.3)	(2098.02)

Next we estimate investment functions for the three different size-classes. The estimated function contains average Q and is supplemented by sales and cash flow, both measured as the ratio to the capital stock.

Table 5.9: Average Q investment functions for class sizes

		$(I/K)_{i,t-1}$	$Q_{i,t-1}$	$(S/K)_{i,t-1}$	$(CF/K)_{i,t-1}$	n
Aggregate	*class 1*	0.0162	0.0771	0.0151	-0.0014	4,480
		(1.07)	(18.75)	(9.43)	(-0.52)	
	class 2	0.1139	0.0516	0.0204	0.0003	4,470
		(7.3)	(13.55)	(9.82)	(0.09)	
	class 3	0.2034	0.0280	0.0285	0.0001	4,470
		(13.38)	(10.68)	(14.02)	(0.02)	
Equipment	*class 1*	0.0111	0.0817	0.0138	-0.0024	4480
		(0.76)	(13.89)	(6.2)	(-0.62)	
	class 2	0.0518	0.0632	0.0244	-0.0054	4,470
		(3.44)	(11.42)	(8.27)	(-1.26)	
	class 3	0.104	0.0395	0.0409	0.0031	4,470
		(6.63)	(8.93)	(11.97)	(0.48)	
Structures	*class 1*	0.0062	0.1244	0.052	0.0038	4,480
		(0.38)	(2.14)	(2.43)	(0.1)	
	class 2	-0.001	0.1002	0.0313	0.0128	4,470
		(-0.06)	(2.22)	(1.34)	(0.36)	
	class 3	0.0823	0.0361	0.028	-0.0934	4,470
		(4.17)	(2.02)	(2.15)	(-3.57)	

It can be seen that the firms belonging to different classes exhibit strong differences in their investment behavior. Turning first to the aggregate investment functions:

The influence of the lagged investment ratio increases considerably from 0.02 for the class of smallest to 0.2 for the class of largest firms and is insignificant different from 0 in the smallest class. Of course, it has to be kept in mind that the smaller the capital stocks the less continuous will the investment process of a firm be according to pure aggregation effects. For larger firms the aggregation will smooth out such discontinuities. The parameter for average Q more than halves from 0.08 for the smallest firms to only 0.03 for the largest firms. Therefore it can be stated that the larger the firms the stronger it's investment ratio is influenced by it's past investment behavior and the less it takes the profitability, measured by average *Q*, into account. Even if *Q* should contain all relevant information, the sales to capital ratio is significant for all classes of firms with parameters roughly equal. This empirical finding, which is present in the most of empirical investment studies, casts doubt on the assumption of perfect competition in product markets.[18]

Because taking the information contained in cash flow into account when calculating *Q*, an overall significance of the cash flow parameter could be seen as indicating the existence of financial constraints.[19] But the cash flow parameter is insignificant in all classes and adds partially only very little to the explanatory power of the investment equation.

It is evident that the explanatory variables help to predict investment in equipment much better compared to investment in structures. Nevertheless, *Q* remains significant in all classes. There is no clear evidence on the role of cash flow. For the smallest and mid-size firms there is no significant influence neither on investment in equipment nor on investment in structures. While the largest firms show positive reaction of investment in equipment on cash flow, there is the opposite effect on investment in structures.

As an interesting result we can state that small firms do not only invest more in average, their investment is to a larger extent determined by profitability and less by last periods investment.

5.3.1.2. Stock measure of internal funds and the cash flow influence

The theoretical discussion in chapter 2 led to the hypothesis that firm's having larger stocks of internal funds at their disposal are less dependent on outside finance and therefore should be less dependent in their investment behavior of cash flow movements.

To test this hypothesis it is necessary to find a proxy indicating the amount of internal funds, which is disposable to finance investment. One prominent balance sheet relation

---

18 This view is supported by the strictily positive public valuation of increases in sales.

19 See Gilchrist and Himmelberg (1998).

used in this way is the ratio of liquidity to the capital stock (Fazzari et al. 1988, Whited 1992). The division through the capital stock does also take account of the pure size effect, which prohibits the use of liquidity as a proxy in levels.

We define the liquidity to capital stock-measure (*LKM*) as the ratio of cash, short-term debtors (less trade debtors) and investments to the capital stock in the year previous to the estimation period to proxy for the availability of internal funds to finance investment:[20]

The following table contains descriptive measures of the liquidity to capital stock-measure for all firms as well as for the firms grouped by firm size:

Table 5.10: Descriptive Statistics, Averages, standard deviation in parentheses

	All	*class 1 (smallest)*	*class 2*	*class 3 (largest)*
n	13,420	4,480	4,470	4,470
LKM	0.365 (0.54)	0.333 (0.57)	0.358 (0.55)	0.405 (0.48)

The descriptive evidence shows that the ratio of internal funds to the capital stock is in average about 0.365. Comparing this figure to the 0.141 average investment ratio means that more than twice of the amount necessary to finance investment could have theoretically been financed by way of internal funds available. Of course this argument does neither take into account the amount of cash necessary to buffer fluctuations in the firm's stream of cash payments nor the firm's ability to cash all debtors. There is no clear relation between the available internal funds and firm size.

In the next step we group firms a priori according to their internal funds measure. According to the theoretical discussion firms having larger internal funds at their disposal should react less on cash flow when deciding about business fixed investment spending. The following table contains descriptive measures. The firms grouped into the

20 The results remain unchanged when using the median of the estimation period as the measure for availability of funds.

class of high internal fund firms have in average a ratio of funds to capital stock three times the average of the low internal fund firms. High internal fund firms have a larger cash flow and sales ratio to the capital stock, too.

Table 5.11: Descriptive measures for low and high liquid firms

	All	class 1 (low)	class 2 (high)
n	13,420	6,710	6,710
I/K	0.141	0.128	0.153
	(0.16)	(0.15)	(0.17)
I^e/K^e	0.203	0.195	0.211
	(0.23)	(0.22)	(0.23)
I^s/K^s	0.182	0.142	0.222
	(1.6)	(1.37)	(1.79)
Q^a	1.517	1.344	1.69
	(1.76)	(1.55)	(1.93)
(S/K)	3.509	2.732	4.285
	(3.57)	(2.07)	(4.47)
(CF/K)	0.155	0.097	0.212
	(0.77)	(0.81)	(0.72)
LKM	0.365	0.186	0.544
	(0.54)	(0.28)	(0.66)

The following table contains the results for all firms as well as for the firms grouped into two classes of firms, high and low internal fund firms in the year previous to the estimation period. For grouping we use the median of the cash to capital stock ratio in the year previous to the estimation period.

Table 5.12: Average Q investment functions for high and low liquid firms

		$(I/K)_{i,t-1}$	$Q^a_{i,t-1}$	$(S/K)_{i,t-1}$	$(CF/K)_{i,t-1}$	n
Aggregate	*low*	0.0222	0.0711	0.0385	-0.0002	6,710
		(1.81)	(21.56)	(17.45)	(-0.11)	
	high	0.0954	0.0487	0.014	0.0006	6,710
		(7.46)	(17.08)	(11.37)	(0.21)	
Equipment	*low*	0.0112	0.0943	0.0401	-0.0045	6,710
		(0.92)	(17.82)	(11.61)	(-1.42)	
	high	0.0612	0.0498	0.0155	0.0023	6,710
		(5.02)	(12.76)	(9.44)	(0.62)	
Structures	*low*	0.0014	0.0444	0.1282	0.0215	6,710
		(0.1)	(1.15)	(5.25)	(0.92)	
	high	0.0055	0.113	0.0284	-0.0004	6,710
		(0.41)	(2.98)	(1.84)	(-0.01)	

The empirical results based on equal size of the a priori groups do not support the hypothesis that firms owning low stocks of liquidity react significantly stronger on cash flow in their investment behavior. Neither for equipment nor for structures is any significant positive cash flow influence evident. The results therefore do not indicate the existence of capital market imperfections, which force low internal fund firms to rely more heavily on cash flow to finance investment.

The method of a priori grouping used was based on a sample splitting into two groups of the same size. Hence it was implicitly assumed that 50 % of all firms face some kind of liquidity constraints. Because there is no theoretical justification to rely on that 50 % value we perform a sensitivity analysis in the following. We use nineteen different quantils for the sample splits, 5 % - 95 %, 10 % - 90 % and so on, to assess the sensitivity of the previous finding to the chosen quantil.

According to the hypothesis stated we expect the difference between the cash flow parameter for the group a priori considered as being stronger constrained to exceed the parameter of the group a priori considered as being less constrained. The following table contains the estimated differences of the cash flow parameter as well as the t-values for these differences when using the nine different quantils for a priori grouping.

Fig. 5.10: Sensitivity analysis of choice of quantils, liquidity, aggregate investment

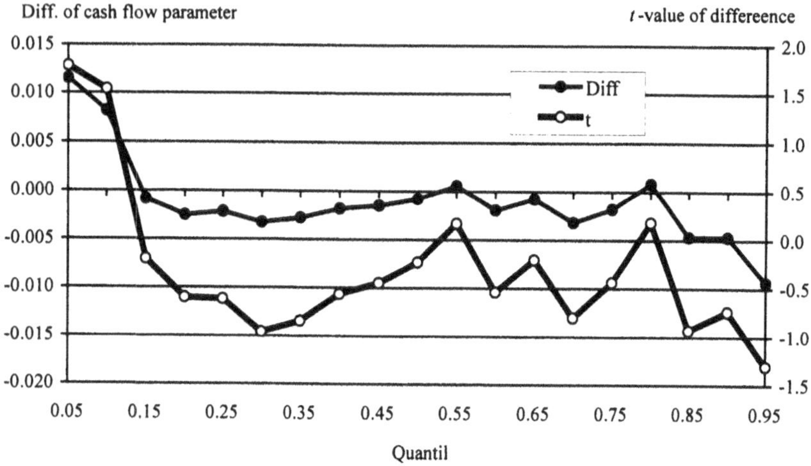

The diagram shows that only the five percent firms having the lowest stock of liquidity react significantly, also only at the ten percent significance level, stronger on cash flow compared to the group of less constrained firms. For all quantils leading to larger groups of constrained firms, we find no notably difference in the cash flow parameter.

Performing the same analysis for the investment in equipment, we find the results depicted in the next figure.

Fig. 5.11: Sensitivity analysis of choice of quantils, liquidity, equipment

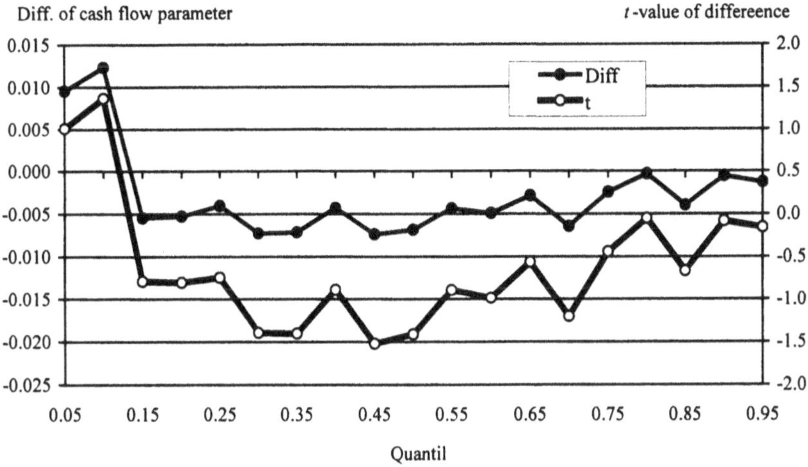

There is for no quantil a significant difference in the cash flow parameter found. Hence we conclude that there is only weak evidence for liquidity constraints when a priori separating the five percent of firms having the lowest liquidity to capital stock measure as liquidity constraint. For investment in equipment only even that evidence disappears.

5.3.1.3. Measures of the bank-relation of firms and the cash flow influence

The theoretical discussion concerning the information costs for firms lead us to state the hypothesis that a close bank-relationship might reduce the information costs due to the state of being under constant monitoring. Therefore firms having close bank relationships might be less dependent on their cash flow when having to finance fixed investment.

To test this hypothesis we use the ratio of long-term bank debt to total debt as the proxy to indicate the strongness of the bank relationship (*BR*). This indicator has the advantage of being independent of the ratio of debt to total assets.

The following table contains descriptive measures of the ratio of long-term bank debt to total debt for all firms as well as for the firms grouped by firm size:

Table 5.13: Descriptive Statistics, Averages, standard deviation in parentheses

	All	*class 1 (smallest)*	*class 2*	*class 3 (largest)*
n	13,420	4,480	4,470	4,470
BR	0.154	0.195	0.155	0.112
	(0.16)	(0.18)	(0.15)	(0.13)

The descriptive evidence shows that the ratio of long-term bank debt to total debt is in average 0.15. For the smaller firms this ratio and, according to our measurement, therefore the bank-relation is stronger compared to larger firms. This evidence is in accordance with the observation that especially smaller firms are more dependent on banks and hence are supported by the rather bank-oriented German financial system.

The following table contains descriptive measures for the two classes of firms having close or loose banking relationships. The firms grouped into the class of closer bank-related firms have in average lower investment ratios and lower *Q*-values.

Table 5.14: Descriptive measures for different degrees of bank relation

	All	class 1 (low)	class 2 (high)
n	13,420	6,720	6,700
I/K	0.141	0.142	0.139
	(0.16)	(0.16)	(0.16)
I^e/K^e	0.203	0.198	0.209
	(0.23)	(0.2)	(0.25)
I^s/K^s	0.182	0.228	0.136
	(1.6)	(1.99)	(1.07)
Q^a	1.517	1.696	1.338
	(1.76)	(1.93)	(1.54)
(S/K)	3.509	4.108	2.908
	(3.57)	(4.43)	(2.27)
(CF/K)	0.155	0.201	0.108
	(0.77)	(0.72)	(0.82)
BR	0.154	0.073	0.235
	(0.16)	(0.11)	(0.16)

The following table contains the results for all firms as well as for the firms grouped into two classes of firms, stronger and less strong bank-related firms in the year previous to the estimation period. For grouping we use the median of the bank relation measure in the year previous to the estimation period.

Table 5.15: Average Q investment functions for high and low bank relation

		$(I/K)_{i,t-1}$	$Q^a_{i,t-1}$	$(S/K)_{i,t-1}$	$(CF/K)_{i,t-1}$	n
Aggregate	*low*	0.0826	0.0550	0.0153	-0.0014	6,710
		(6.34)	(19.79)	(12.67)	(-0.56)	
	high	0.051	0.0612	0.028	0.0019	6,710
		(4.14)	(18.24)	(13.84)	(0.87)	
Equipment	*low*	0.0257	0.0539	0.0172	-0.0045	6,710
		(2.06)	(14.57)	(10.94)	(-1.34)	
	high	0.0437	0.0866	0.0325	0.0022	6,710
		(3.62)	(16.16)	(10.29)	(0.63)	
Structures	*low*	0.0047	0.1461	0.0373	0.0302	6,710
		(0.35)	(3.39)	(2.12)	(0.77)	
	high	0.0069	0.0115	0.0569	0.0025	6,710
		(0.5)	(0.4)	(3.46)	(0.13)	

When splitting the sample of firms into groups of firms according to the bank relation, the results do not support the hypothesis stated, that firms classified as closer bank related react significantly less on cash flow and hence could be seen as less liquidity constraint. Neither for less nor for stronger bank related firms do we find a significant cash flow influence. While less bank related firms react to a smaller degree on Q^a compared to closer bank related firms when investing in equipment the opposite result is found for investment in structures.

The results present in the table relied on the a priori grouping using the median of the indicator for bank relation. To assess the sensitivity of the previous finding to the chosen quantil we use different quantils in the following.

The theoretical reasoning did not lead to a clear out hypothesis about the difference between the cash flow parameter for the group a priori considered as being less and stronger bank related. The following table contains the estimated differences of the cash flow parameter as well as the *t*-values for these differences when using the nineteen different quantils for a priori grouping.

Fig. 5.12: Sensitivity analysis of choice of quantils, bank relation, aggregate investment

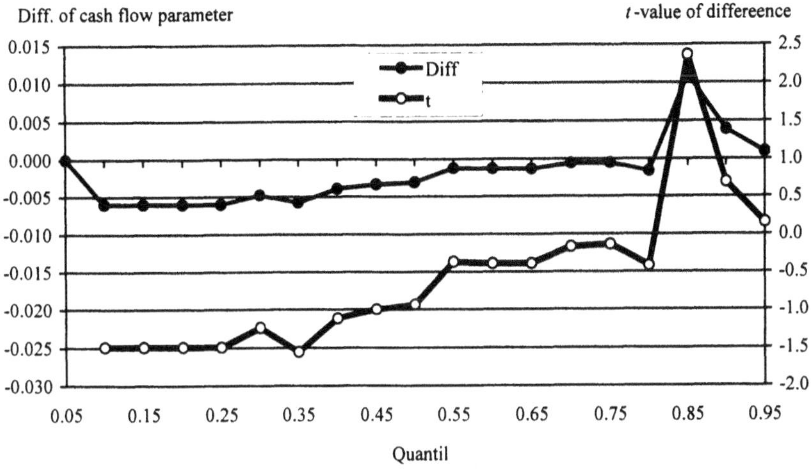

The diagram shows the findings for different quantils. When splitting the sample by the median or quantils in the neighborhood of the median, there is no difference in the cash flow parameter between firms having low and high shares of bank debt to total debt. But the more firms we include into the group of less bank related firms, the higher the difference in the cash flow parameter, only the result using the 85 %-quantil can be seen as an outlier because the steady increase of the difference is interrupted and the parameter value as well as the t-value jumps to an significant *t*-value. Altogether the small group of less bank related firms reacts less positive or even negative on cash flow compared to the larger group of closer bank related firms. If we use quantils that lead to a small group of stronger bank related firms, we find that these firms react less on cash flow. But because for no quantil we find a significant positive reaction for neither of the two groups under consideration. Hence, there is no evidence for liquidity constraints.

Performing the same analysis for the investment in equipment, we find the results depicted in the next figure.

Fig. 5.13: Sensitivity analysis of choice of quantils, bank relation, equipment

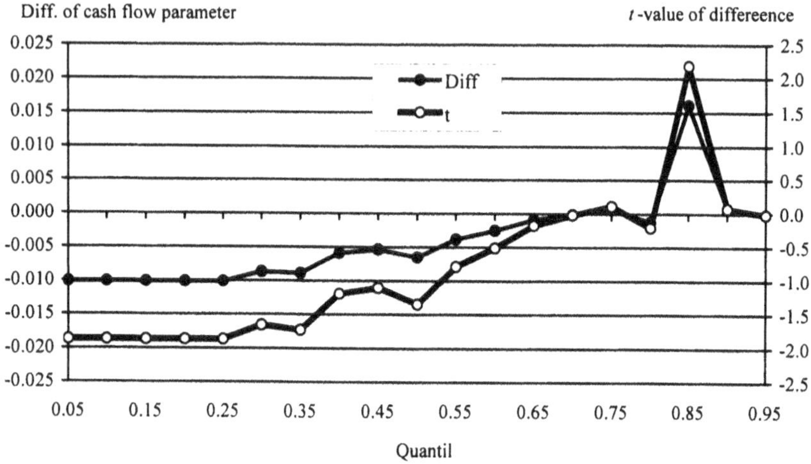

The finding for investment in equipment is very similar to the findings for aggregate investment. Again we find an outlier when using the 85 %-quantil for a priori grouping of firms. Because there is no positive cash flow influence in the two groups considered making use of different quantils for the a priori grouping, we conclude that there is no evidence for lesser or stronger bank related firms being liquidity constraint.

5.3.1.4. Debt service of firms and the cash flow influence

In this chapter we want to test the hypothesis that debt service has a negative effect on investment beyond the fact that cash payment commitments reduce cash flow. The reasoning is that lenders might interpret high debt payments as a bad signal concerning potential insolvency. Furthermore firms having compulsory large debt service might face agency costs arising from asymmetric information (Myers/Mayluf, 1984), and contract enforcement problems (Jensen/Meckling 1986). According to Jensen/Meckling (1976) debt financing might create an incentive to choose investment projects to risky because of limited liability. In an empirical investigation Ndikumana (1999) found the debt service to have a negative impact on investment when analyzing U.S. firm level panel data.

To test this hypothesis we use the ratio of interest expense to the capital stock to measure the degree of debt service (*DS*) the firm is obliged to.[21]

The following table contains descriptive measures of the ratio of interest expense to the capital stock for all firms as well as for the firms grouped by firm size:

Table 5.16: Descriptive Statistics, Averages, standard deviation in parentheses

	All	*class 1 (smallest)*	*class 2*	*class 3 (largest)*
n	13,420	4,480	4,470	4,470
DS	0.051 (0.06)	0.060 (0.07)	0.053 (0.06)	0.039 (0.04)

The descriptive evidence shows that the ratio of debt service to the capital stock is in average 0.051. For the smaller firms this ratio is 54% higher compared to the ratio for larger firms. This evidence confirms the observation that smaller firms rely to a higher degree on outside finance compared to larger firms.

The following table contains descriptive measures for the two classes of firms having high and low ratios of debt service. The firms grouped into the class of high debt service firms have in average higher investment ratios, lower Q^a-values and especially a higher sales productivity of its capital stock. For high debt service firms the ratio of interest expense to the capital stock is more than three times the ratio of low debt service firms.

21 Ndikumana (1999) uses beside the the ratio of interest expense to the capital stock the ratio of interest expense to the sum of interest expense and cash flow (p. 470). But because cash flow is negative in almost ten percent of firm years, we regard the last indicator as inappropriate.

Table 5.17: Descriptive measures for different degrees of debt service

	All	class 1 (low)	class 2 (high)
n	13,420	6,710	6,710
I/K	0.141	0.126	0.155
	(0.16)	(0.13)	(0.18)
I^e/K^e	0.203	0.189	0.218
	(0.23)	(0.2)	(0.25)
I^s/K^s	0.182	0.125	0.239
	(1.6)	(1.16)	(1.93)
Q^a	1.517	1.585	1.449
	(1.76)	(1.9)	(1.6)
(S/K)	3.509	2.665	4.352
	(3.57)	(1.95)	(4.5)
(CF/K)	0.155	0.175	0.134
	(0.77)	(0.56)	(0.93)
DS	0.051	0.025	0.076
	(0.06)	(0.02)	(0.07)

The following table contains the regression results for all firms as well as for the low and high debt service firms.[22]

22 For grouping we use the median of the debt service ratio in the year previous to the estimation period.

Table 5.18: Average Q investment functions for high and low debt service firms

		$(I/K)_{i,t-1}$	$Q^a_{i,t-1}$	$(S/K)_{i,t-1}$	$(CF/K)_{i,t-1}$	n
Aggregate	*low*	0.1308	0.0432	0.0257	0.0014	6,710
		(9.94)	(17.35)	(12.61)	(0.54)	
	high	0.0428	0.0704	0.0164	-0.0017	6,710
		(3.48)	(19.83)	(12.7)	(-0.77)	
Equipment	*low*	0.0632	0.0505	0.0311	-0.0045	6,710
		(5.04)	(12.97)	(9.93)	(-1.07)	
	high	0.0274	0.0798	0.0168	-0.0015	6,710
		(2.29)	(15.86)	(9.38)	(-0.49)	
Structures	*low*	0.0017	0.0747	-0.0067	0.0575	6,710
		(0.12)	(2.7)	(-0.31)	(1.94)	
	high	0.0075	0.1209	0.0555	-0.0115	6,710
		(0.56)	(2.55)	(3.4)	(-0.39)	

When splitting the sample of firms into groups of firms according to the debt service ratio, we find no support for the hypothesis stated, that firms facing high debt service react stronger on cash flow.[23] Neither aggregate investment nor the investment in equipment is strongly influenced by the cash flow for both groups of firms. Only low debt service facing firms react statistically significant when investing in structures. Firms facing high debt service payments react stronger on Q^a when deciding about investment in structures as well as in equipment.

To assess the sensitivity of the previous finding to the chosen median we use different quantils for the a priori grouping in the following.

Because theoretical reasoning led to the hypothesis that high debt service firms should be at more risk to face liquidity constraints, we expect a negative difference between the cash flow parameter for the low debt service group and the cash flow parameter for the

---

23 This result is confirmed when using the debt service ratio as an additional regressor directly. The parameter appears insignificant.

high debt service firms. The following figure contains the estimated differences of the cash flow parameter as well as the *t*-values for these differences when using the nine different quantils for a priori grouping.

Fig. 5.14: Sensitivity analysis of choice of quantils, debt service, aggregate investment

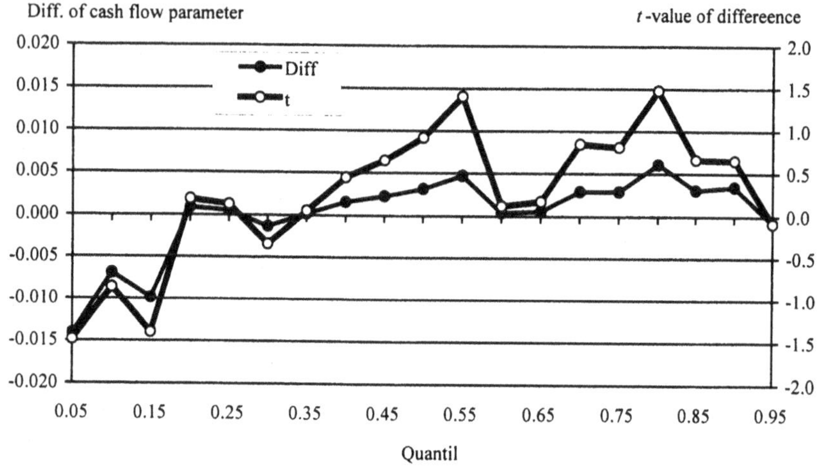

We find that no splitting leads to a significant difference in the cash flow parameter. This finding is in accordance with no cash flow parameter for any of the groups is positive significant.

Performing the same analysis for the investment in equipment, we find the results depicted in the next figure.

Fig. 5.15: Sensitivity analysis of choice of quantils, equipment

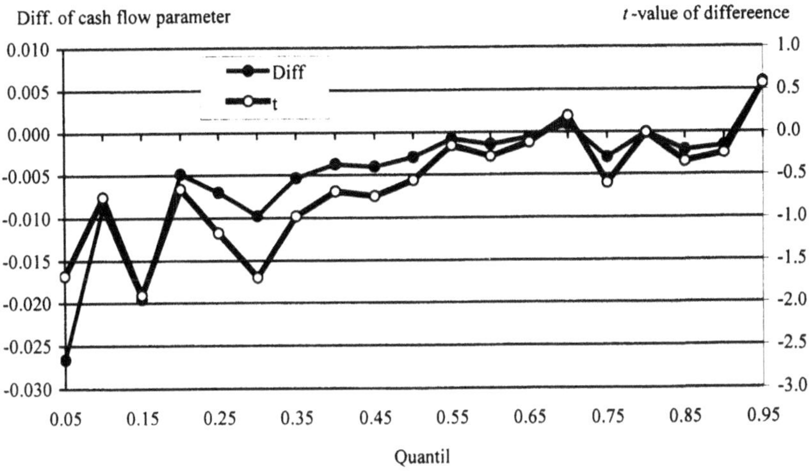

The finding for investment in equipment seems to be in accordance with the hypothesis stated. Low debt service firms react less on the cash flow when deciding about investment in equipment. But because there is no positive cash flow influence in the two groups considered for any quantils used for the a priori grouping, we conclude that there is no evidence for higher debt service firms being liquidity constraint. The insignificant but negative parameters for most groups is not corresponding to any theoretical reasoning. Hence, the results give no support for the hypotheses stated that high debt service firms have less access to capital for financing investment and hence have to rely to a larger extent on cash flow.

5.3.1.5. Conclusion

In this chapter we tested several hypotheses stating that firms beeing in a state of liquidity constraintness react stronger on their cash flow when deciding about investment. The data basis contained 1,342 manufacturing firms covering the twelve years for the period of 1987 to 1998.

Q^a should make use of all information contained in the cash flow that helps to predict future profitability. Therefore the cash flow is interpreted as indicating the change in available internal sources to finance investment. Only when firms face some constraints on external finance of profitable investment projects the cash flow should exercise some significant influence on investment.

The estimation results of dynamic investment equations showed Q^a to influence the firm's fixed investment spending significantly. When supplementing the Q-investment equation by sales and cash flow the sales variable turned out to influence investment significantly while there was now isolated cash flow influence. This result confirms most empirical findings in the framework of the Q-theory concerning the prevailing influence of sales, which could be seen as indicating the existence of economies of scale. While the cash flow appears significantly in most empirical investment analysis, we attribute our opposite empirical finding of absence of cash flow as evidence for the reliability of our Q^a measure.

The information cost considerations predict firms having low internal funds at their disposal being subject to financial constraints. Using a measure of internal funds, this prediction was not confirmed in the empirical analysis. Firms classified as having less internal funds at their disposal reacted even less on cash flow, opposite to what should have been expected according to the model of hierarchy of the costs of finance.

The issue of monitoring through banks was analyzed using a measure of bank-relation. There is the wide held view that firms having closer bank-relationships do react less strongly to their cash flow. Our empirical findings do not support the hypothesis that constant monitoring through banks helps firms to lower the informational asymmetries and thereby ease the financing of profitable investment projects.

Because often it is argued that firms facing a high debt service have less access to finance investment through outside finance, finally the role of the debt service ratio was analyzed. Again the empirical results do not show any evidence for a stronger cash flow dependence of high debt service firms supposed to face financial constraints.

While these results clearly support the Q-theory of investment, no evidence for the hypothesis that firms supposed to face severe liquidity constraints according to the information and adverse selection theory was found. Hence the questions concerning the existence and the manner of working of the balance sheet channel remain open for future research.

5.3.2. Liquidity effects in construction firms investment behavior

In the previous chapter we analyzed the liquidity effects on manufacturing firms. In this chapter we now turn to analyze, using the same method, the investment behavior of construction firms. The database contains 112 construction firms, which differ considerable concerning the balance sheet structure from manufacturing firms.

The following dynamic Q-investment equation is supplemented by sales (S) as well as the cash flow (CF).

Q-investment function for aggregate investment

$$\widehat{\left(\frac{I}{K}\right)_t} = a_i + \underset{(2.90)}{0.0876}\left(\frac{I}{K}\right)_{t-1} + \underset{(6.95)}{0.0501}\, Q^a_{t-1} + \underset{(7.34)}{0.0246}\left(\frac{S}{K}\right)_{t-1} - \underset{(-1.67)}{0.0083}\left(\frac{CF}{K}\right)_{t-1}$$

$n = 1{,}120$

The cash flow parameter is - opposite to what could be expected - negative. But t-value indicates that the parameter is not significant different from 0 and compared to the t-values of the other variables the parameter is rather estimated imprecisely. Like it was found for manufacturing firms, the sales variable indicates that there is still some relevant information in sales not captured by the measure of Q. The three regressors, lagged investment, average Q and sales are strongly significant and reveal roughly the same partial correlation to the investment ratio. When comparing the lower t-values, especially for Q^a, for construction firms, it has to be considered that the degrees of freedom differ considerably; hence we should expect the parameters of the investment equation for manufacturing firms to be estimated more precisely.

Next we estimate investment functions separately for equipment and structures.

Q-investment function for investment in equipment

$$\widehat{\left(\frac{I^e}{K^e}\right)_t} = a_i \underset{(-1.14)}{-0.0314}\left(\frac{I^e}{K^e}\right)_{t-1} \underset{(4.42)}{+0.0400}\, Q^a_{t-1} \underset{(5.34)}{+0.0252}\left(\frac{S}{K}\right)_{t-1} \underset{(-0.66)}{-0.0047}\left(\frac{CF}{K}\right)_{t-1}$$

$n = 1{,}120$

Q-investment function for investment in structures

$$\widehat{\left(\frac{I^s}{K^s}\right)_t} = a_i \underset{(-0.36)}{-0.0113}\left(\frac{I^e}{K^e}\right)_{t-1} \underset{(2.40)}{+0.2026}\, Q^a_{t-1} \underset{(1.55)}{+0.0652}\left(\frac{S}{K}\right)_{t-1} \underset{(-1.17)}{-0.0761}\left(\frac{CF}{K}\right)_{t-1}$$

$n = 1{,}120$

While we find that Q^a and sales exert significant positive influence on investment in equipment, the investment in structures of construction firms cannot be explained adequately using our approach. No parameter is significantly different from 0. Hence we have to conclude the investment in structures is determined by factors exogenous to the supplemented *Q*-investment function.

5.3.2.1. Stock measure of internal funds and the cash flow influence

Being the case that only investment in equipment is sufficiently explained using the *Q*-approach, in the following we restrict the analysis for construction firms on their investment in equipment.

To test the hypothesis that construction firms having large stocks of liquidity at their disposal, react less on cash flow in their investment behavior, we group according to the liquidity to capital stock-measure.[24]

The following table contains descriptive measures. The firms grouped into the class of high internal fund firms have in average a ratio of funds to capital stock three times the

---

24 We define the liquidity to capital stock-measure (*LKM*) as the ratio of cash, short term debtors (less trade debtors) and investments to the capital stock in the year previous to the estimation period to proxy for the availability of internal funds to finance investment. See also chapter 6.2.

average of the low internal fund firms. High internal fund firms have a larger cash flow and sales ratio to the capital stock, too.

Table 5.19: Descriptive measures for low and high liquid firms

	All	class 1 (low)	class 2 (high)
n	1120	560	560
I^e/K^e	0.286	0.28	0.293
	(0.27)	(0.27)	(0.27)
Q^a	1.201	1.072	1.331
	(1.94)	(1.5)	(2.29)
S/K	4.364	3.212	5.516
	(3.22)	(2.35)	(3.55)
CF/K	0.137	0.101	0.174
	(1.03)	(0.87)	(1.18)
LKM	0.937	0.401	1.474
	(1.25)	(0.51)	(1.51)

The following table contains the results for all firms as well as for the firms grouped into two classes of firms, high and low internal fund firms in the year previous to the estimation period. For grouping we use the median of the cash to capital stock ratio in the year previous to the estimation period. The table shows that high and low liquid firms have approximately the same investment ratio, but high liquid firms have considerable higher sales and cash flow to capital stock ratios.

Table 5.20: Average Q investment functions for high and low liquid firms

		$(I/K)_{i,t-1}$	$Q^a_{i,t-1}$	$(S/K)_{i,t-1}$	$(CF/K)_{i,t-1}$	n
Equipment	*low*	0.0155	0.0995	0.0599	-0.0082	560
		(0.4)	(4.82)	(5.22)	(-0.68)	
	high	-0.0968	0.031	0.0249	-0.0076	560
		(-2.53)	(3.04)	(4.74)	(-0.9)	

The regression results are not in accordance with the hypothesis stated, that firms having less stocks of liquidity at their disposal react significantly on cash flow and less on Q^a compared to firms having larger stocks of liquidity at their disposal. The Q^a-parameter is approximately the same for both groups of firms, while the cash flow, opposite what was expected based on the theoretical considerations, exerts insignificant negative influence on investment in equipment.

5.3.2.2. Measures of the bank-relation of firms and the cash flow influence

To test the hypothesis that a close bank-relationship might reduce the information costs due to the state of being under constant monitoring we use the ratio of long-term bank debt to total debt as the proxy to indicate the strongness of the bank relationship (*BR*). This indicator has the advantage of being independent of the ratio of debt to total assets.

The following table contains descriptive measures for the two classes of construction firms having close and lesser close banking relationships. The firms grouped into the class of closer bank-related firms have in average lower investment ratios and lower Q^a-values.

Table 5.21: Descriptive measures for different degrees of bank relation

	All	class 1 (low)	class 2 (high)
n	1120	560	560
I^e/K^e	0.286	0.29	0.283
	(0.27)	(0.26)	(0.27)
Q^a	1.201	1.101	1.302
	(1.94)	(2.18)	(1.66)
S/K	4.364	5.148	3.58
	(3.22)	(3.77)	(2.31)
CF/K	0.137	0.157	0.118
	(1.03)	(1.18)	(0.87)
BR	0.079	0.034	0.124
	(0.11)	(0.06)	(0.12)

The following table contains the results for all firms as well as for the firms grouped into two classes of firms, stronger and less strong bank-related firms in the year previous to the estimation period. For grouping we use the median of the bank relation measure in the year previous to the estimation period.

Table 5.22: Average Q investment functions for high and low bank relation

		$(I/K)_{i,t-1}$	$Q^a_{i,t-1}$	$(S/K)_{i,t-1}$	$(CF/K)_{i,t-1}$	n
Equipment	*low*	-0.0919	0.0419	0.0252	0.0018	560
		(-2.36)	(3.89)	(4.71)	(0.21)	
	high	0.0205	0.0411	0.025	-0.016	560
		(0.52)	(2.5)	(2.47)	(-1.3)	

When splitting the sample of firms into groups of firms according to the bank relation, the results do partially support the hypothesis stated, that firms classified as closer bank related show less signs of being liquidity constraint. Firms classified as stronger bank related react stronger on Q^a as well as on sales in their investment spending. The negative partial influence of cash is not in accordance with theory.

5.3.2.3. Debt service of firms and the cash flow influence

In this chapter we want to test the hypothesis that debt service has a negative effect on investment beyond the fact that cash payment commitments reduce cash flow. To test this hypothesis we use the ratio of interest expense to the capital stock to measure the degree of debt service (*DS*) the firm is obliged to.

The following table contains descriptive measures for the two classes of firms having high and low ratios of debt service. The firms grouped into the class of high debt service firms have in average higher investment ratios, similar Q^a-values and especially a higher sales productivity of its capital stock. For high debt service firms the ratio of interest expense to the capital stock is more than three times the ratio of low debt service firms.

Table 5.23: Descriptive measures for different degrees of debt service

	All	*class 1 (low)*	*class 2 (high)*
n	1120	560	560
I^e/K^e	0.286	0.264	0.309
	(0.27)	(0.23)	(0.3)
Q^a	1.201	1.142	1.261
	(1.94)	(2.05)	(1.82)
(S/K)	4.364	3.541	5.187
	(3.22)	(2.03)	(3.91)
(CF/K)	0.137	0.164	0.111
	(1.03)	(0.82)	(1.21)
DS	0.05	0.023	0.077
	(0.05)	(0.02)	(0.06)

The following table contains the regression results for all firms as well as for the low and high debt service firms.[25]

Table 5.24: Average Q investment functions for high and low bank relation

		$(I/K)_{i,t-1}$	$Q^a_{i,t-1}$	$(S/K)_{i,t-1}$	$(CF/K)_{i,t-1}$	n
Equipment	*low*	-0.071	0.0309	0.0193	-0.0079	560
		(-1.68)	(2.21)	(1.75)	(-0.63)	
	high	-0.0044	0.0472	0.0252	-0.0017	560
		(-0.12)	(3.89)	(4.56)	(-0.19)	

When splitting the sample of firms into groups of firms according to the debt service ratio, we find that firms facing high debt service react stronger on sales and less on Q^a.[26] For neither group of firms investment is strongly influenced by the cash flow.

5.3.2.4. Conclusion

In this chapter we analyzed the investment behavior of 112 German construction firms. The framework of the Q-theory only showed satisfying results for the investment in equipment, while the Q-model has no explanatory power on investment in structures. Hence we concentrated on firms' investment in equipment when analyzing the cash flow influence.

The estimation results of dynamic investment equations showed Q^a to influence the firm's fixed investment spending significantly. When supplementing the Q-investment equation by sales and cash flow the sales variable turned out to influence investment significantly while there was now isolated cash flow influence. This result confirms the results obtained for manufacturing firms.

---

25 For grouping we use the median of the debt service ratio in the year previous to the estimation period.

26 This result is confirmed when using the debt service ratio as an additional regressor directly. The parameter appears insignificant.

We proceeded with an a priori grouping of firms according to indicators which were chosen based on theoretical considerations to discriminate between firms facing different degrees of financial constraints. We expected firms having lower stocks of liquidity, weak bank-relationship and high debt service to react less on Q^a and stronger on cash flow in their investment decision. While the hypothesis stated for reduced influence of Q^a was confirmed by the regression results, we found no evidence that firms a priori considered as facing stronger financial constraints react significantly stronger on cash flow.

5.3.3. Liquidity effects in commerce firms investment behavior

In the two previous chapters we analyzed the liquidity effects on manufacturing and construction firms. In this chapter we now turn to analyze the investment behavior of commerce firms. The database contains 860 commerce firms, which differ considerable concerning the balance sheet structure from manufacturing firms.

The following dynamic Q-investment equation is supplemented by sales (S) as well as the cash flow (CF).

Q-investment function for aggregate investment

$$\widehat{\left(\frac{I}{K}\right)_t} = a_i + \underset{(0.74)}{0.0084}\left(\frac{I}{K}\right)_{t-1} + \underset{(15.49)}{0.0468}\, Q^a_{t-1} + \underset{(16.67)}{0.0079}\left(\frac{S}{K}\right)_{t-1} + \underset{(0.26)}{0.0005}\left(\frac{CF}{K}\right)_{t-1}$$

$n = 8{,}600$

Like it was found for manufacturing and construction firms, the sales variable indicates that there is still some relevant information in sales not captured by the measure of Q^a. The average Q parameter is strongly significant and reveals roughly the same partial correlation to the investment ratio as the sales variable. Neither lagged investment nor cash flow influence the aggregate investment spending of commerce firms significantly.

Next we estimate investment functions separately for equipment and structures.

Q-investment function for investment in equipment

$$\widehat{\left(\frac{I^e}{K^e}\right)_t} = a_i \underset{(-1.92)}{-0.0211}\left(\frac{I^e}{K^e}\right)_{t-1} \underset{(11.37)}{+0.0549}\, Q^a_{t-1} \underset{(7.72)}{+0.0056}\left(\frac{S}{K}\right)_{t-1} \underset{(0.97)}{+0.0031}\left(\frac{CF}{K}\right)_{t-1}$$

$n = 8{,}600$

Q-investment function for investment in structures

$$\widehat{\left(\frac{I^s}{K^s}\right)_t} = a_i \underset{(-0.09)}{-0.0010}\left(\frac{I^e}{K^e}\right)_{t-1} \underset{(0.97)}{+0.0310}\, Q^a_{t-1} \underset{(8.19)}{+0.0386}\left(\frac{S}{K}\right)_{t-1} \underset{(-0.96)}{-0.0203}\left(\frac{CF}{K}\right)_{t-1}$$

$n = 8{,}600$

We find that Q^a and sales exert significant positive influence on investment in equipment, the investment in structures of commerce firms cannot be adequately explained by the investment equation. Sales only influence the investment in structures significantly. Because of these regression results we analyze investment in equipment in greater detail only.

5.3.3.1. Stock measure of internal funds and the cash flow influence

To test the hypothesis that construction firms having large stocks of liquidity at their disposal, react less on cash flow in their investment behavior, we group according to the liquidity to capital stock-measure.[27]

The following table contains descriptive measures for the two groups of firms according to the liquidity to capital stock-measure.[28]

---

27 We define the liquidity to capital stock-measure (*LKM*) as the ratio of cash, short term debtors (less trade debtors) and investments to the capital stock in the year previous to the estimation period to proxy for the availability of internal funds to finance investment. See also chapter 6.2.

28 We define the liquidity to capital stock-measure (*LKM*) as the ratio of cash, short term debtors (less trade debtors) and investments to the capital stock in the year previous to the estimation period to proxy for the availability of internal funds to finance investment. See also chapter 6.2.

The firms grouped into the class of high internal fund firms have in average a ratio of funds to capital stock almost five times the average of the low internal fund firms. High internal fund firms have a larger cash flow and sales ratio to the capital stock as well as higher Q^a-values, too.

Table 5.25: Descriptive measures for low and high liquid firms

	All	*class 1 (low)*	*class 2 (high)*
n	8,600	4,300	4,300
I^e/K^e	0.282	0.279	0.286
	(0.3)	(0.31)	(0.29)
Q^a	1.76	1.536	1.983
	(1.86)	(1.56)	(2.09)
S/K	10.045	5.442	14.647
	(10.93)	(4.79)	(13.17)
CF/K	0.133	0.050	0.216
	(1.1)	(0.97)	(1.21)
LKM	0.551	0.202	0.901
	(0.97)	(0.27)	(1.24)

The following table contains the results for all firms as well as for the firms grouped into two classes of firms, high and low internal fund firms in the year previous to the estimation period. For grouping we use the median of the cash to capital stock ratio in the year previous to the estimation period. The table shows that high and low liquid firms have approximately the same investment ratio, but high liquid firms have considerable higher sales and cash flow to capital stock ratios.

Table 5.26: Average Q investment functions for high and low liquid firms

		$(I/K)_{i,t-1}$	$Q^a_{i,t-1}$	$(S/K)_{i,t-1}$	$(CF/K)_{i,t-1}$	n
Equipment	*low*	0.0125	0.0812	0.0124	0.0049	4300
		(0.8)	(8.91)	(4.99)	(0.95)	
	high	-0.071	0.0407	0.0055	0.0018	4300
		(-4.57)	(7.22)	(7.15)	(0.43)	

The regression results confirm the hypothesis stated, that firms having less stocks of liquidity at their disposal react significantly on cash flow opposite to firms having larger stocks of liquidity at their disposal. The Q^a-parameter is equally significant in both groups but higher in value for low liquid firms. While sales are highly significant in both groups of firms, lagged investment exerts a significant partial influence for high liquid firms.

5.3.3.2. Measures of the bank-relation of firms and the cash flow influence

To test the hypothesis that a close bank-relationship might reduce the information costs due to the state of being under constant monitoring we use the ratio of long-term bank debt to total debt as the proxy to indicate the strongness of the bank relationship (*BR*). This indicator has the advantage of being independent of the ratio of debt to total assets.

The following table contains descriptive measures for the two classes of construction firms having close and lesser close banking relationships. The firms grouped into the class of closer bank-related firms have in average considerably higher Q^a-values, sales and cash flow values. The share of long-term bank debt to total debt is more than twice the ratio for close related firms compared to less related firms.

Table 5.27: Descriptive measures for different degrees of bank relation

	All	class 1 (low)	class 2 (high)
n	8600	4300	4300
I^e/K^e	0.282	0.277	0.287
	(0.3)	(0.29)	(0.31)
Q^a	1.76	1.815	1.704
	(1.86)	(2)	(1.7)
S/K	10.045	12.607	7.482
	(10.93)	(12.22)	(8.73)
CF/K	0.133	0.174	0.092
	(1.1)	(1.12)	(1.08)
BR	0.125	0.054	0.196
	(0.15)	(0.1)	(0.16)

The following table contains the results for all firms as well as for the firms grouped into two classes of firms, stronger and less strong bank-related firms in the year previous to the estimation period. For grouping we use the median of the bank relation measure in the year previous to the estimation period.

Table 5.28: Average Q investment functions for high and low bank relation

		$(I/K)_{i,t-1}$	$Q^a_{i,t-1}$	$(S/K)_{i,t-1}$	$(CF/K)_{i,t-1}$	n
Equipment	*low*	-0.0414	0.0477	0.0053	0.0044	4300
		(-2.63)	(7.62)	(6.01)	(1.01)	
	high	-0.0065	0.0639	0.0071	0.0019	4300
		(-0.42)	(8.5)	(5.5)	(0.41)	

The regression results for the two groups of firms, classified according to their bank relation, show no signs of firms being liquidity constraint and resemble in the regression parameters for Q^a and sales. Hence, we find no strong difference in the investment behavior of firms with different ratios of bank debt.

5.3.3.3. Debt service of firms and the cash flow influence

In this chapter we want to test the hypothesis that debt service has a negative effect on investment beyond the fact that cash payment commitments reduce cash flow. To test this hypothesis we use the ratio of interest expense to the capital stock to measure the degree of debt service (*DS*) the firm is obliged to.

The following table contains descriptive measures for the two classes of firms having high and low ratios of debt service. The firms grouped into the class of high debt service firms have in similar investment ratios but higher Q^a-values and especially a higher sales productivity of its capital stock. The average cash flow to capital stock ratio is also twice the ratio of low debt service firms. For high debt service firms the ratio of interest expense to the capital stock is more than four times the ratio of low debt service firms.

Table 5.29: Descriptive measures for different degrees of debt service

	All	*class 1 (low)*	*class 2 (high)*
n	8600	4300	4300
I^e/K^e	0.282	0.28	0.284
	(0.3)	(0.3)	(0.3)
Q^a	1.76	1.609	1.91
	(1.86)	(1.82)	(1.87)
(S/K)	10.045	5.627	14.463
	(10.93)	(5.48)	(13.03)
(CF/K)	0.133	0.09	0.175
	(1.1)	(0.83)	(1.32)
DS	0.111	0.044	0.178
	(0.14)	(0.03)	(0.16)

The following table contains the regression results for all firms as well as for the low and high debt service firms.[29]

Table 5.30: Average Q investment functions for high and low debt service

		$(I/K)_{i,t-1}$	$Q^a_{i,t-1}$	$(S/K)_{i,t-1}$	$(CF/K)_{i,t-1}$	n
Equipment	*low*	0.0155	0.0611	0.0165	-0.0021	4300
		(0.98)	(7.85)	(6.43)	(-0.34)	
	high	-0.0765	0.0492	0.0055	0.0046	4300
		(-5.03)	(8.13)	(7.26)	(1.26)	

When splitting the sample of firms into groups of firms according to the debt service ratio, we find that firms facing high debt service react stronger on cash flow, but the cash flow effect is not statistically significant.[30] For both groups of firms we find a similar Q^a-influence, while low debt service firms react considerably stronger on sales.

5.3.3.4. Conclusion

In this chapter we analyzed the investment behavior of 8,600 German commerce firms. The framework of the Q-theory only showed satisfying results for the investment in equipment, while the Q^a-variable has no explanatory power on investment in structures. Hence we concentrated on firms' investment in equipment when analyzing the cash flow influence.

The estimation results of dynamic investment equations showed Q^a to influence the firm's fixed investment spending significantly. When supplementing the Q-investment equation by sales and cash flow the sales variable turned out to influence investment significantly while there was less evidence for an isolated cash flow influence. This

---

[29] For grouping we use the median of the debt service ratio in the year previous to the estimation period.

[30] This result is confirmed when using the debt service ratio as an additional regressor directly. The parameter appears insignificant.

result is in accordance with the results obtained for manufacturing and construction firms.

We proceeded with an a priori grouping of firms according to indicators which were chosen based on theoretical considerations to discriminate between firms facing different degrees of financial constraints. We expected firms having lower stocks of liquidity, weak bank-relationship and high debt service to react less on Q^a and stronger on cash flow in their investment decision. While the hypothesis of significant cash flow influence on liquidity constraint firms only was confirmed when using the stock of liquidity for grouping, we found no relevant cash flow influence when analyzing the bank relation and the debt service ratio.

5.4. An analysis of size effects

In this chapter we concentrate on the effect of firm size on the link of liquidity constraints and investment.

5.4.1. Introduction

There is often some affection for small firms observed and especially attempts to promote the financing of small firms are popular. At the moment in Germany there is some ongoing discussion about smaller firms ("Mittelstand") to be financially constraint because of tightened credit policy of banks. Tax reductions as well as easing credit restrictions are by many politicians seen as one way to support smaller firms especially and to stimulate their investment. In this context the question arises whether there is a failure in financial markets that limits the investment behavior of small firms.[31]

In the discussion of liquidity constraints and its effect on firms investment the firm size plays a crucial role. Often firm size is used as an a priori indicator for the existence of liquidity constraints, based on the assumption that small firms have less access to capital (Fazzari/Hubbard/Petersen 1988). Therefore through analyzing the cash flow effect within different classes of firm size the hypothesis that firms face some form of liquidity constraints and hence the hypothesis of a perfect capital market is tested.

---

31 See Weinberg (1994).

Audretsch and Elston (2002) analyzed size effects on the investment behavior of German firms within the framework of the Q-model based on a small sample of 100 stock quoted firms. Taking special emphasis on the role of firm size the authors found ambiguous evidence for the effect of firm size and cash flow on investment.

Our aim is to add further evidence on the relation between cash flow and investment and the interaction with firm size, as small firms are often seen as the driving force of growth on the one hand but suffering from financial constraints on the other hand.

In Germany bank loans play a crucial role in financing firm's investment and the dependency on bank loans increases in average with smaller firm size. The descriptive evidence shows that the ratio of long-term bank debt to total debt is in average 0.14 for all firms in the sample. When splitting the data set according to firm size, measured as balance sheet total assets, into three classes, we find that the smallest firms have a ratio of 0.160 while it is only 0.105 for the largest firms. Therefore the bank-relatedness can be said to be stronger for small firms compared to larger firms.

The relying on intermediation by banks might add a cost component to the costs of financing investment. On the other hand the close relationship of German firms to their financing banks can be seen as a constant process of monitoring that could lead to a reduction of the problem of asymmetric information. Thereby the negative effect of firm size on the access to liquidity might be offset by the positive monitoring effect. This might make the assumption of small firms being more liquidity constrained questionable for German firms. Indeed has it been argued that this special institutional feature of the German financial system precludes liquidity constraints to occur (Cable 1985). Of course, monitoring is not costless and these additional costs again might, even for the case of reduced asymmetric information, drive a wedge between internal and external costs of finance.

Using the Q theory approach, the effect of firm size on liquidity constraints of German firms has been analyzed by Audretsch and Elston (2002). But as mentioned above, this empirical study was based on a small sample of 100 quoted firms only. In their study Audretsch and Elston got rather dissatisfying results concerning the explanatory power of Q^a. In only one out of the three size classes, firms were found to react significantly on Q^a. While small firms, opposed to what could have been assumed, showed no significant reaction, especially medium-sized firms were found to be cash flow dependent in their investment spending. The inclusion of firm size as an explanatory variable led to inconclusive regression results, too. The impact of size on small and large firms has been positive while the influence was found negative for medium-sized firms.

5.4.2. Aggregate investment and firm size effects

We start the empirical analysis using the complete data set covering three main sectors: manufacturing, construction and commerce. The firm individual Q^a-variable was calculated separately within the three different sectors making use of a panel-VAR.

The following dynamic investment equations are estimated using a direct bias correction method[32] and contains beside Q^a sales (S) as well as the cash flow (CF).[33]

$$\widehat{\left(\frac{I}{K}\right)_t} = a_i + \underset{(9.26)}{0.0626}\left(\frac{I}{K}\right)_{t-1} + \underset{(32.24)}{0.0548}\, Q^a_{t-1} + \underset{(21.79)}{0.0081}\left(\frac{S}{K}\right)_{t-1} + \underset{(0.78)}{0.0009}\left(\frac{CF}{K}\right)_{t-1}$$

$n = 23{,}140$

The cash flow parameter appears insignificant but the sales variable indicates that there is still some relevant information in sales not captured by the measure of Q^a. The measure of profitability (Q^a) is by far more powerful in explaining investment behavior compared to sales and cash flow. We interpret the result therefore as supporting evidence for the Q theory of investment. The results do not hint for the presence of an independent cash flow influence.[34]

Next we test whether firm size, measured as real balance sheet total assets at the beginning of period (RTA), effects investment significantly. Therefore the investment equation is supplemented with the logarithm of the real balance sheet total.

---

32 For details see Hansen (2001) and Behr/Bellgardt (2002).

33 The comparable LSDV and GMM estimates are contained in the appendix.

34 In the context of a user cost model including several lags, von Kalckreuth (2001) and Chirinko and von Kalckreuth (2002) found a significant cash flow influence indicating the existence of liquidity constraints for German firms.

$$\widehat{\left(\frac{I}{K}\right)}_t = a_i + \underset{(13.31)}{0.0769}\left(\frac{I}{K}\right)_{t-1} + \underset{(27.63)}{0.0483}\,Q^a_{t-1} + \underset{(22.13)}{0.0082}\left(\frac{S}{K}\right)_{t-1}$$

$$+ \underset{(1.08)}{0.0013}\left(\frac{CF}{K}\right)_{t-1} - \underset{(-14.57)}{0.0743}\ln RTA_{t-1} \qquad n = 23{,}140$$

We find that firm size has a strong and significant negative effect on investment, while the empirical results for the other variables resemble. In the following we split the data set into sub samples according to firm size.

5.4.3. Firm size effects on investment

The following table contains descriptive evidence for the three size classes according to the firm's total assets.

Table 5.31: Descriptive statistics for classes by firm size

(mean, standard deviation in parentheses)

	All	*class 1 (smallest)*	*class 2*	*class 3 (largest)*
n	23,140	7,720	7,710	7,710
I/K	0.145	0.165	0.143	0.128
	(0.18)	(0.22)	(0.17)	(0.13)
Q^a	1.592	1.792	1.518	1.465
	(1.81)	(1.91)	(1.71)	(1.77)
S/K	5.979	8.253	5.317	4.365
	(7.88)	(10.55)	(6.26)	(5.24)
CF/K	0.146	0.105	0.15	0.182
	(0.92)	(1.22)	(0.79)	(0.66)
RTA	126.442	4.185	15.843	359.458
	(959.94)	(2.84)	(9.31)	(1638.38)

It can be seen that the investment ratio is highest for the smallest of firms (almost 16.5%), while it is just below 13% for the largest firms. The smallest firms show the highest profitability measured through Q^a as well as the highest sales to capital ratio. The cash flow per unit of capital is in contrast well below average for the smallest of firms.

Table 5.32: Average Q investment functions for class sizes

(parameter, *t*-value in parentheses)

	All	*class 1 (smallest)*	*class 2*	*class 3 (largest)*
n	23,140	7,720	7,710	7,710
$(I/K)_{i,t-1}$	0.0626	0.0252	0.0635	0.152
	(9.26)	(2.16)	(5.4)	(13.13)
$Q^a_{i,t-1}$	0.0548	0.0701	0.0544	0.0331
	(32.24)	(21.45)	(17.87)	(15.06)
$(S/K)_{i,t-1}$	0.0081	0.006	0.0136	0.0105
	(21.79)	(10.55)	(17.31)	(13.31)
$(CF/K)_{i,t-1}$	0.0009	-0.0022	0.0029	-0.001
	(0.78)	(-1.05)	(1.22)	(-0.51)

When estimating dynamic investment functions for each of the three different classes of firms, we find several remarkable results. The larger the firms, the less its investment is influenced by Q^a while its dependence on lagged investment increases.[35]

Concerning the cash flow influence we find somewhat unexpected that only mid-sized firms reacting on cash flow with increasing investment. For no group of firms the cash flow parameter is statistically significant. A similar pattern, that mid-sized firms only exhibit cash-flow sensitivity, was found by Audretsch and Elston (2002) using a different database and stock market data.

35 This effect might be of cause in part due to the fact that several overlapping investment projects within larger firms will smooth out discontinuities.

Especially the finding that the smallest firms show no reaction in investment spending to changes in their net wealth contradicts the prediction of the information cost-model. According to the theoretical predictions of the model of asymmetric information especially small firms should have the greatest informational disadvantages leading to high information costs when depending on outside finance.

It is also worth asking, whether firm size, measured as real total assets (*RTA*), has a direct influence on investment activity.[36] While the descriptive evidence suggests such a relation, which was also found in the aggregate investment function, in the multivariate context the partial effect of firm size on investment cannot be inferred from the average investment rates in different size-classes. The next table contains the estimated investment functions, further supplemented by lagged firm size.

Table 5.33: Q-investment functions and the direct influence of firm size

(parameter, *t*-value in parentheses)

	All	*class 1 (smallest)*	*class 2*	*class 3 (largest)*
n	23,140	7,720	7,710	7,710
$(I/K)_{i,t-1}$	0.0769	0.0403	0.0827	0.1618
	(11.3)	(3.44)	(6.97)	(13.92)
$Q^a_{i,t-1}$	0.0483	0.0624	0.0469	0.0288
	(27.63)	(18.58)	(14.95)	(12.66)
$(S/K)_{i,t-1}$	0.0082	0.0061	0.0137	0.0108
	(22.13)	(10.84)	(17.56)	(13.71)
$(CF/K)_{i,t-1}$	0.0013	-0.0016	0.0028	-0.0013
	(1.08)	(-0.79)	(1.16)	(-0.64)
$\ln RTA_{i,t-1}$	-0.0743	-0.0978	-0.0823	-0.0463
	(-14.57)	(-9.39)	(-9.45)	(-7.13)

36 See the appendix for data description.

When analyzing the firms belonging to different classes, the firm size itself shows a strong negative influence in all three classes. This means that the negative partial relation between firm size and investment is present within all classes of firms. The firm size-parameter as well as its significance decreases for larger firms. Again, no group of firms displays a significant reaction to cash flow.

5.4.4. A sectoral analysis of firm size effects

Because the analysis so far was based on the data file containing firms of three very distinct broad sectors, manufacturing, construction and commerce, the value of the results presented so far may be questioned because of the very distinct features of firms belonging these different sectors. To investigate the existence of sectoral effects we split the data set according to these three main sectors.

The following table contains descriptive measures, the unweighted mean of firm individual rates and the standard deviation thereof. Firms belonging to different sectors are up to quite different production technologies and probably different investment behavior.

Table 5.34: Descriptive statistics by sectors

(mean, standard deviation in parentheses)

	All	*Manufact.*	*Construct.*	*Commerce*
n	23,140	13,420	1,120	8,600
I/K	0.145	0.141	0.171	0.149
	(0.18)	(0.16)	(0.18)	(0.2)
Q^a	1.592	1.517	1.201	1.76
	(1.81)	(1.76)	(1.94)	(1.86)
S/K	5.979	3.509	4.364	10.045
	(7.88)	(3.57)	(3.22)	(10.93)
CF/K	0.146	0.155	0.137	0.133
	(0.92)	(0.77)	(1.03)	(1.10)
RTA	126.442	175.348	209.561	39.302
	(959.94)	(1232.03)	(758.44)	(154.3)

It can be seen that the sales to capital ratio for commerce is almost three times the ratio of manufacturing and construction firms. While the sector construction has the highest investment ratio (17.1%), it has the lowest Q^a, in average just about 1.2. The fact that construction firms are more than five times and manufacturing firms still 4.5 times larger than commerce firms is remarkable and means that a grouping by size has mainly the effect of varying shares of sectors in different classes by size. The following table contains the shares of these three sectors in the different classes by firm size.

The cross table makes evident, that the class of smallest firms contains a majority of firms belonging to the sector commerce (55%), while the class of largest firms contains mainly manufacturing firms (73%) and only 21% commerce firms.

Table 5.35: Share of sectors in classes by size

Share of sectors	*All*	*class 1 (smallest)*	*class 2*	*class 3 (largest)*
Manufacturing	0.58	0.41	0.60	0.73
Construction	0.05	0.04	0.05	0.06
Commerce	0.37	0.55	0.35	0.21
All sectors	1	1	1	1

In the following we estimate dynamic investment functions for the three sectors separately. It is evident that firms in each sector react most strongly on Q^a. The effect of lagged investment is not significant for commerce firms while the influence is quite strong for manufacturing and construction firms. Even after controlling for investment opportunities through Q^a, sales influences investment significantly in all sectors. The cash flow variable which is often seen as the variable indicating the existence of financial market frictions has no significant explanatory power for manufacturing firms and commerce firms while it has even an unreasonable small negative influence on construction firms' investment.

Table 5.36: Average Q investment functions for sectors

(parameter, t-value in parentheses)

	All	*Manufact.*	*Construct.*	*Commerce*
n	23,140	13,420	1,120	8,600
$(I/K)_{i,t-1}$	0.0626	0.0738	0.0876	0.0084
	(9.26)	(8.30)	(2.90)	(0.74)
$Q^a_{i,t-1}$	0.0548	0.0568	0.0501	0.0468
	(32.24)	(26.62)	(7.86)	(15.49)
$(S/K)_{i,t-1}$	0.0081	0.018	0.0246	0.0079
	(21.79)	(17.65)	(7.34)	(16.67)
$(CF/K)_{i,t-1}$	0.0009	-0.0003	-0.0083	0.0005
	(0.78)	(-0.20)	(-1.67)	(0.26)

When adding real total assets as an explanatory variable, we find that the strong negative effect of firm size on investment is present within the sectors manufacturing and commerce.

For construction firms only the negative effect is insignificant. The previous findings for the cash flow resemble. There is no significant positive effect of cash flow present that could be interpreted as indicating financial constraints.

Table 5.37: Average Q investment functions for sectors containing real firm size

(parameter, t-value in parentheses)

	All	*Manufact.*	*Construct.*	*Commerce*
n	23,140	13,420	1,120	8,600
$(I/K)_{i,t-1}$	0.0769	0.0921	0.0903	0.0189
	(11.3)	(10.28)	(2.97)	(1.67)
$Q^a_{i,t-1}$	0.0483	0.0485	0.0496	0.0395
	(27.63)	(21.79)	(7.71)	(12.79)
$(S/K)_{i,t-1}$	0.0082	0.0184	0.0247	0.0081
	(22.13)	(18.12)	(7.35)	(17.18)
$(CF/K)_{i,t-1}$	0.0013	-0.0001	-0.0089	0.0017
	(1.08)	(-0.07)	(-1.76)	(0.85)
$\ln RTA_{i,t-1}$	-0.0743	-0.0789	-0.0113	-0.0909
	(-14.57)	(-12.58)	(-0.59)	(-9.83)

5.4.5. Summarizing the size effects

In this chapter we analyzed size effects in the investment behavior of German firms within the framework of the Q-theory. Because of using anonymous individual firm balance sheet data, no stock market measure of Q is available. The database contained 2,314 firms covering the twelve years for the period of 1987 to 1998.

When examining the effect of size on investment behavior, the investment ratio of German firms is found to be significantly negative related to firm's total assets. This surprisingly strong effect is present even within classes of different size and within the sector of manufacturing firms as well as in the sector of commerce.

While the study led to strong evidence on a significant negative effect of firm size on investment, the results concerning the cash flow influence do not suggest the existence of severe liquidity constraints giving raise to an important balance sheet channel for monetary effects.

In view of the theoretical discussion of information costs, the finding that even the smallest of firms are not subject to liquidity constraints is surprising but in accordance with results of Audretsch and Elston (2002). One possible explanation might be the special features of the German bank-based financial system being especially supportive for the smallest of firms.

5.5. An eclectic approach

In the previous chapter we took special emphasis on the role of cash flow on investment. According to theoretical considerations we explored whether firms, grouped a priori as having less facilities to finance new investment, show stronger reaction to cash flow. The results were not favorable to this financial constraint hypothesis indicating no significant partial cash flow influence. The indicators used to classify firms are well known balance sheet ratios, known to be under consideration when analyzing balance sheets.

In this chapter a different approach is chosen, namely we directly analyze whether the investment ratio of firms correlates partially with the balance sheet ratios used as indicators for a priori grouping in the previous chapters.

We base our analysis on the sectoral data set for the sectors, manufacturing, construction and commerce. To take account of heterogeneity we add fixed firm- and year-effects to. By estimating the investment function separately we allow the parameters for the explanatory variables to take different values in each of the three main sectors.

The balance sheet ratios we consider are the following:

- *LMK*: the ratio of liquidity to the capital stock at replacement costs
- *BR*: the ratio of long-term bank dept to total dept indicating the tightness of bank relation
- *DS*: the ratio of interest payments to the capital stock at replacement costs
- *DR*: the ratio of debt to balance sheet total

Based on the results on the previous chapters indicating a strong influence of the firm size we consider additionally the real balance sheet total (*RTA*).

The investment function to estimate is:

$$\left(\frac{I}{K}\right)_t = a_i + \lambda_t + \beta_1 \left(\frac{I}{K}\right)_{t-1} + \beta_2\, Q^a_{t-1} + \beta_3 \left(\frac{S}{K}\right)_{t-1} + \beta_4 \left(\frac{CF}{K}\right)_{t-1} + \beta_4 \log(RTA)_{t-1}$$

$$+ \beta_6\, LMK_{t-1} + \beta_7\, BR_{t-1} + \beta_8\, DS \left(\frac{CF}{K}\right)_{t-1} + \beta_9\, DR \left(\frac{CF}{K}\right)_{t-1} + \varepsilon_{it}$$

The following table contains the results for the bias corrected estimates:

We find that investment is apart from investment in the commerce sector strongly positive dependent on last years investment. Sales still partially influences investment significantly in all sectors, even when controlling for investment opportunities via Q^a. Due to the much higher sales per capital ratio in the commerce sector, the parameter is considerably smaller in that sector.

In no sector we find any hint for a partially relevant influence of cash flow on investment. This in view of the extended literature discussing the influence liquidity on investment is the most remarkable result.

Table 5.38: Supplemented average Q investment functions for sectors

(parameter, t-value in parentheses)

	All	*Manufact.*	*Construct.*	*Commerce*
n	23,140	13,420	1,120	8,600
$(I/K)_{i,t-1}$	0.0782	0.0961	0.0965	0.0205
	(11.57)	(10.82)	(3.21)	(1.82)
$(S/K)_{i,t-1}$	0.0066	0.0155	0.0194	0.0063
	(15.28)	(14.70)	(5.35)	(11.19)
$(CF/K)_{i,t-1}$	0.0003	-0.0021	-0.0071	0.0014
	(0.29)	(-1.29)	(-1.4)	(0.71)
$Q^a_{i,t-1}$	0.0449	0.0447	0.0508	0.0375
	(25.61)	(19.97)	(7.72)	(12.08)
$\ln RTA_{i,t-1}$	-0.0771	-0.0853	-0.0215	-0.091
	(-14.67)	(-13.12)	(-1.08)	(-9.44)
$LMK_{i,t-1}$	0.0349	0.0445	0.0334	0.025
	(13.8)	(11.87)	(3.69)	(6.45)
$BR_{i,t-1}$	-0.1289	-0.0971	-0.301	-0.1366
	(-10.65)	(-7.00)	(-4.25)	(-6.01)
$DS_{i,t-1}$	-0.0083	-0.1352	-0.007	0.0769
	(-0.32)	(-2.84)	(-0.04)	(2.16)
$DR_{i,t-1}$	-0.1129	-0.1244	-0.3522	-0.0611
	(-7.04)	(-7.11)	(-3.77)	(-1.82)

As was already evident in chapter 5 is also in this extended regression approach to assert: small is beautiful. In the manufacturing as well as in the commerce sector we find a strong negative partial relation between firm size and investment.

Turning to the balance sheet ratios indicating the availability of liquidity and the facilities to finance investment via outside finance, we find that three out of the four hypotheses under consideration are strongly supported by the empirical finding. We find that

- firms having larger stocks of liquidity at their disposal tend to investment more.

- firms having large debt ratios tend to invest less

- manufacturing firms facing high debt service ratios tend to invest less (but the opposite is found for commerce firms).[37]

The results also indicate that firms having larger shares of their debt financed by long-term bank loans tend to invest less. Concerning this point the theoretical considerations were inconclusive because the state of stronger monitoring could be seen as information asymmetries reducing and hence facilitating the access to finance. On the other hand the interpose of intermediaries might also induce higher costs compared to direct access to capital markets and hence could reduce investment via higher costs of finance. The results therefore hint for the second effect to predominate.

Altogether the findings question the adequacy of the a priori approach to test for differences in effects of cash flow on investment. Almost no significant cash flow effects in neither group of firms, whether expected to be financial constraint or not, was evident in the a priori grouping approach. Nevertheless when testing for a direct influence of balance sheet ratios on investment the empirical findings confirm to a large extend the hypothesis stated based on theoretical considerations.

While this significant influence of several balance sheet ratios as well as of firm size and sales on investment is not in accordance with the neoclassical Q-theory of investment, assuming Q to be a sufficient statistic for investment. It would have been overoptimistic to assume that in practice such a complex decision like investment could be explained empirically solely by one measure of investment opportunities. Taking into account the heterogeneity of 2,314 under consideration, the very strong results for average Q are satisfying. The significance of further determinants of investment found in the investment regressions should not be seen as to unexpected taking into account the practical use of balance sheet ratios when decisions about financing investment are made.

---

37 These results confirm findings by Fazzari and Athey (1987) and Ndikumana (1999) who found for US firms a negative effect of the debt ratio and the debt service ratio on investment. See p. 471.

6. Summary

In our analysis we applied the Q-theory of investment to a large sample of German firms and to explore the role of financial factors in the firm's investment decision. The analysis was based on balance sheet data for 2,314 German firms, thereof 1,342 manufacturing firms, giving the unique opportunity to analyze heterogeneity at the firm level.

The Q-theory of investment was used as the theoretical basis because this theory derives explicitly from an optimization problem the firms' investment determination. The strong assumptions necessary to derive a linear relationship between the ratio of investment to the capital stock and a measure of Q are naturally not fulfilled in a one to one manner when turning to an empirical application. The deviations in empirical investment research from the theoretical forecasts, especially from the dichotomy between real investment and the financing issues due to the assumption of perfect capital markets, evoked doubts on the theoretical assumptions.

In several empirical analyses firms in a weak financial position were found to be unable to raise capital at conditions that allow financing all profitable investment projects and hence were found to depend on internal liquidity.

There are two possible and competing explanations for the additional variable's significance, especially liquidity measures and sales. Often these findings, especially the significance of cash flow in investment regressions, are taking as evidence for the existence of capital market imperfections. But the measurement problems of Tobin's Q can cause low explanatory power of Tobin's Q itself and significant coefficients of other explanatory variables. In this context it is obvious, that the less accurate Q is proxied by the variable used in regression analysis the less clear is the interpretation of the regression results. The more the proxy used deviates from the correct Q, the more space is left for cash flow to be significant for measuring investment opportunities beyond measuring pure changes in net wealth.

In view of this discussion in our analysis we took special emphasis on the measurement problems arising when making use of balance sheet data to explore investment behavior. First we used a complex procedure to calculate reliable replacement values of the firm's capital stock and second we used a vector autoregressive approach (VAR) for panel data to estimate present values of the future profitabilities of capital to calculate Q. The achievement of this direct forecasting approach is the applicability of the Q-theory to non-quoted firms as well.

In chapter four we discussed several linear dynamic panel data estimators proposed in the literature. It is a well-known fact that the natural choice, the least squares dummy variable estimator is biased in the context of dynamic estimation. The estimators taking into account the resulting bias can be grouped broadly into the class of instrumental estimators and the class of direct bias corrected estimators. Because there are now various estimators available, the applied researcher faces the problem of choosing among these. While in empirical applications instrumental estimators are widely used, our simulation results seem to favor direct bias corrected methods.

The results contained by making use of the direct bias correction method show a very strong and significant influence of the calculated marginal Q as well as of average Q based on balance sheet data on firm's investment. The very strong influence of the Q-measures was found in all of the three broad sectors, manufacturing, construction and commerce, considered. The two different Q-measures, we found to be partially only weakly correlated, both have strong and significant explanatory power for investment. In all sectors investment is positively related to lagged investment hinting for gradual adjustments to the optimal capital stock.

Because the investment behavior of manufacturing firms is expected to differ from the investment behavior of construction and commerce firms, these sectors are in the following analyzed separately. In this chapter we study the effects of liquidity on manufacturing firms investment decisions in depth.

To explore the influence of liquidity on investment the approach based on an a priori grouping of firms according to their disposition to face financial constraints was followed. The influence of additional explanatory variables is rather low compared to the strong influence of the Q-measure; nevertheless we find significant parameters for sales. While a significant cash flow parameter is often found in empirical research and usually seen as indicating the existence of liquidity constraints our empirical results do not indicate any relevant cash flow influence when controlling for investment opportunities via Q.

The information cost considerations predict firms having low internal funds at their disposal being subject to financial constraints. Using a measure of internal funds, this prediction was not confirmed in the empirical analysis. Firms classified as having less internal funds at their disposal reacted even less on cash flow, opposite to what should have been expected according to the model of hierarchy of the costs of finance.

The issue of monitoring through banks was analyzed using a measure of bank-relation. There is the wide held view that firms having closer bank-relationships do react less strongly to their cash flow. Our empirical findings do not support the hypothesis that constant monitoring through banks helps firms to lower the informational asymmetries and thereby ease the financing of profitable investment projects.

Because often it is argued that firms facing a high debt service have less access to finance investment through outside finance, finally the role of the debt service ratio was analyzed. Again the empirical results do not show any evidence for a stronger cash flow dependence of high debt service firms supposed to face financial constraints.

While these results clearly support the *Q*-theory of investment, no evidence for the hypothesis that firms facing severe liquidity constraints react strongly on cash flow, according to the information and adverse selection theory, was found in the a priori grouping approach. Hence the questions concerning the existence and the manner of working of the balance sheet channel remain open for future research.

In an additional analysis we took up the question of the influence of the firm size on the investment decision. Concerning the role of firm size we got a very clear result in our analysis: "Small is beautiful". We found that firm size, measured as balance sheet total, is strongly negative correlated to the investment ratio. This remarkably result was confirmed when disaggregating the database in different directions. We found the strong negative influence of firm size to be present when turning to a sectoral analysis as well as when grouping the firms into classes if size.

While in the a priori grouping approach we only had analyzed whether different firms, grouped according to balance sheet ratios, react differently on cash flow, we also asked whether there is a direct partial correlation between investment and balance sheet ratios indicating the financial situation of the firm. Opposite to the results in the a priori grouping approach we found that the results were strongly in accordance with the theoretical considerations. We found that firms having large stocks of liquidity at their disposal tend to investment more, while firms having large debt ratios and a larger share of long-term bank debt tend to invest less. The expected negative effect of debt service was found for manufacturing only.

Altogether we conclude that the direct forecasting approach facilitates the application of the *Q*-theory of investment to firm level balance sheet data. The derived *Q* measures are strongly significant related to the investment ratio. Concerning the influence of liquidity we found no partial correlation of cash flow and investment when controlling for investment opportunities via *Q*. We attribute this finding to the satisfying measurement of *Q*. The effect of cash flow on investment was also absent when splitting the sample a priori into groups considered to face different access to finance. Whether our finding of significant influence of several balance sheet ratios, known to be practically used in financing decisions, should be interpreted as influencing the investment decision because containing relevant information about future profits or via different facilities of outside financing remains an open question for future research.

Appendix

A. An empirical comparison of several proposed dynamic panel data estimators

In this section we want to apply the discussed estimators to a large firm level panel data set and return to the simulation results, especially to assess the case of endogeneity of x in face of the empirical results. The model to estimate is a dynamic average Q^a investment function.[1] The variable to be explained is the investment ratio, while the explanatory variable is from the beginning of period Q^a, which is hence the case of a predetermined variable.

In this section we apply the discussed estimators to the manufacturing data file described above. We estimate a dynamic investment function including average Q^a as the regressor beside the lagged investment ratio.

$$\left(\frac{I}{K}\right)_{it} = a_i + \rho\left(\frac{I}{K}\right)_{i,t-1} + \beta\, Q^a_{it-1} + \varepsilon_{it}$$

Table A.1 contains the empirical results.

Leaving aside the pooled estimator, which is clearly not appropriate, and the least square dummy variable estimator known to be biased, we still find a large amount of variation in the estimates. The estimates of ρ range from 0.075 for the Anderson-Hsaio estimator using lagged differences as instruments to 0.176 for the bias corrected estimator proposed by Hansen. The parameters for Q^a show some variation, too. The lowest estimate is obtained using the GMM estimators proposed by Arellano and Bond while the highest parameter value results for the Anderson-Hsiao estimator using lagged differences as instruments.

---

1 For an exact description of the variables see sections 4.2. and 4.3.

Table A.1: Empirical results of the dynamic Q-investment function

	ρ	$std(\rho)$	$t(\rho)$	β	$std(\beta)$	$t(\beta)$
γ^{Pooled}	0.243	0.008	29.73	0.015	0.001	17.73
γ^{LSDV}	0.072	0.009	8.47	0.106	0.003	39.84
$\gamma^{AH,L}$	0.107	0.016	6.73	0.141	0.004	36.4
$\gamma^{AH,D}$	0.075	0.022	3.48	0.174	0.005	37.75
$\gamma^{BC,H}$	0.176	0.009	20.58	0.104	0.003	38.86
$\gamma^{BC,K1}$	0.145	0.016	8.87	0.096	0.008	11.74
$\gamma^{BC,K2}$	0.167	0.010	17.43	0.101	0.006	16.35
γ^{GMM1}	0.128	0.016	7.89	0.043	0.003	16.71
γ^{GMM2}	0.165	0.008	20.26	0.042	0.001	29.93
γ^{SYS1}	0.106	0.009	12.44	0.102	0.003	38.06
γ^{SYS2}	0.109	0.009	12.75	0.101	0.003	37.96

We now turn to the problem of potential endogeneity of the Q-variable. As was found in the simulation results this endogeneity of Q, even in the case of predetermination, could lead to the conclusion that the system estimator proposed by Blundell and Bond should be favored. To judge the seriousness of the problem in the empirical data, we estimate the following regression equation for Q^a:

$$Q_{it}^{a} = a_i + \rho\left(\frac{I}{K}\right)_{i,t-1} + \beta\, Q_{it-1}^{a} + \varepsilon_{it}$$

Table A.2: Empirical results for the regression of Q^a on lagged values

	ρ	$std(\rho)$	$t(\rho)$	β	$std(\beta)$	$t(\beta)$
γ^{Pooled}	0.23	0.009	25.19	0.008	0.001	9.12
γ^{LSDV}	0.055	0.01	5.5	0.011	0.001	7.06
$\gamma^{AH,L}$	0.159	0.022	7.08	0.000	0.002	-0.09
$\gamma^{AH,D}$	0.135	0.028	4.77	0.001	0.002	0.33
$\gamma^{BC,H}$	0.202	0.01	19.84	0.011	0.002	7.41
$\gamma^{BC,K1}$	0.156	0.02	7.92	-0.011	0.004	-2.63
$\gamma^{BC,K2}$	0.171	0.016	11.00	-0.008	0.003	-2.38
γ^{GMM1}	0.166	0.02	8.49	-0.018	0.005	-3.95
γ^{GMM2}	0.209	0.013	16.54	-0.001	0.003	-0.49
γ^{SYS1}	0.093	0.01	9.27	0.010	0.001	6.62
γ^{SYS2}	0.130	0.009	14.5	0.018	0.003	5.89

We find that Q^a is significantly related to its lagged value, the parameter is in average about 0.15. The lagged investment ratio does not seem to influence Q^a significantly. The different estimators are in average about 0 with varying signs.

This empirical finding leads us to the conclusion that the problem of endogeneity in the data is not very serious. Hence the use of a GMM or system estimator instead of the somewhat superior direct bias corrected estimators is not indicated by the empirical findings.[2]

The final estimate making use of the bias corrected estimator based on the quadratic minimization is:

---

2 When using the investment ratio of the same period as the variables used to construct Q^a, the results resemble. The parameters of the investment ratio have varying signs and have in average a very small negative value with low *t*-values.

$$\left(\frac{I}{K}\right)_{it} = a_i + \underset{(20.58)}{0{,}176}\left(\frac{I}{K}\right)_{i,t-1} + \underset{(38.86)}{0{,}104}\; Q_{i,t-1} + \hat{\varepsilon}_{it}$$

We find that Q^a influences the investment decision of German manufacturing firms most significantly. The actual investment ratio is also depends significantly positive on last year's investment ratio. This finding shows that the dynamic estimation in this empirical case is appropriate.

Reviewing to the empirical comparison, we find that the different estimators lead to the same conclusions concerning the investment behavior of German manufacturing firms based on the Deutsche Bundesbank's Corporate Balance Sheet Statistics. Investment is strongly positive dependent on lagged investment and Q^a. Nevertheless, in detail the differences of the estimated parameters are not negligible.

To analyze the potential problems caused by endogeneity in the empirical data, the influence of investment on Q^a was assessed by estimating a dynamic equation. The results do not indicate that the endogeneity in this empirical example is serious. Hence the use of direct corrected estimators as well as the system estimator seems appropriate. The resemblance of the results obtained by the direct bias corrected and the system estimator also support this conclusion.

B. GMM and LSDV Estimates

In this appendix we present for comparability GMM, GMM-System and LSDV estimates for manufacturing firms. We instrument lagged investment ratio only by making use of all valid instruments. Because two-step GMM estimates are known to have unreliable estimates of the standard deviation, we show one-step results only. According to the Sargan-Test all instrumented estimations display the problem of overidentifying restrictions. For reasons of comparability we did not experiment with different lag length and different sets of instruments.

GMM Estimates

$$d\widehat{\left(\frac{I}{K}\right)} = \underset{(4.37)}{0.064}\, d\left(\frac{I}{K}\right)_{-1} + \underset{(14.20)}{0.113}\, dQ_{i,t-1} \qquad n = 10{,}736$$

Sargan p-value 0.000, AR(2) p-value 1.000.

GMM-System Estimates

$$d\widehat{\left(\frac{I}{K}\right)} = \underset{(2.41)}{0.039}\, d\left(\frac{I}{K}\right)_{-1} + \underset{(12.90)}{0.021}\, dQ_{i,t-1} \qquad n = 12{,}078$$

Sargan p-value 0.000, AR(2) p-value 0.186.

LSDV Estimates

$$\widehat{\frac{I}{K}} = \underset{(2.75)}{0.037}\left(\frac{I}{K}\right)_{-1} + \underset{(30.a9)}{0.064}\, dQ_{i,t-1} \qquad n = 13{,}420$$

GMM-Estimates containing sales and cash flow

$$d\widehat{\left(\frac{I}{K}\right)} = \underset{(3.14)}{0.053}\, d\left(\frac{I}{K}\right)_{-1} + \underset{(13.60)}{0.115}\, dQ_{i,t-1} + \underset{(0.30)}{0.001}\, d\left(\frac{S}{K}\right)_{-1} - \underset{(-0.44)}{0.004}\, d\left(\frac{CF}{K}\right)_{-1} \qquad n = 10{,}736$$

Sargan p-value 0.000, AR(2) p-value 0.799.

GMM-System-Estimates (Arellano/Bond 1998) containing sales and cash flow

$$d\widehat{\left(\frac{I}{K}\right)} = \underset{(1.56)}{0.025}\, d\left(\frac{I}{K}\right)_{-1} + \underset{(10.80)}{0.018}\, dQ_{i,t-1} + \underset{(4.58)}{0.005}\, d\left(\frac{S}{K}\right)_{-1} + \underset{(2.50)}{0.020}\, d\left(\frac{CF}{K}\right)_{-1} \qquad n = 12{,}078$$

Sargan p-value 0.000, AR(2) p-value 0.363.

LSDV-Estimates containing sales and cash flow

$$\widehat{\frac{I}{K}} = -\underset{(-3.08)}{0.027}\left(\frac{I}{K}\right)_{-1} + \underset{(26.05)}{0.055}\, Q^{a}_{i,t-1} + \underset{(21.55)}{0.022}\left(\frac{S}{K}\right)_{-1} + \underset{(0.05)}{0.000}\left(\frac{CF}{K}\right)_{-1} \qquad n = 13{,}420$$

References

Abel, Andrew B./Blanchard, Olivier J. (1986), The Present Value of Profits and Cyclical Movements in Investment, Econometrica 54, March, p. 249-274.

Akerlof, George A. (1970), The Market for Lemmons: Quality Uncertainty and the Market Mechanism, Quarterly Journal of Economics, Vol. 83, No. 3, p. 488-500.

Anderson, T. W./Hsiao, Cheng (1981), Estimation of Dynamic Models With Error Components, Journal of the American Statistical Association, Vol. 76, No. 375, p. 598-606.

Anderson, T.W./Hsiao, C. (1982): Formulation and estimation of dynamic models using panel data, Journal of Econometrics, Vol. 18, p. 47-82.

Arellano, M. (1989): A note on the Anderson-Hsiao estimator for panel data, Economics Letters, Vol. 31, p. 337-341.

Arellano, Manuel/Bond, Steven (1991), Some Tests of Specifications for Panel Data: Monte Carlo Evidence and an Application to Employment Equations, The Review of Economic Studies, Vol. 58, April, p. 277-298.

Audretsch, David B./Elston, Julie A. (2002), Does firm size matter? Evidence on the impact of liquidity constraints on firm investment behavior in Germany, International Journal of Industrial Organization, Vol. 20, No. 1, p. 1-17.

Baltagi, Badi H. (2001): Econometric Analysis of Panel Data, 2nd edition, Chichester.

Barnett, Steven A./Sakellaris, Plutarchos (1998), Nonlinear response of firm investment to Q: Testing a model of convex and non-convex adjustment costs, Journal of Monetary Economics, Vol. 42, p. 261-288.

Behr, Andreas/Bellgardt, Egon (1998), Sektorale Investitionsentwicklung und Liquiditätseinfluss, Kredit und Kapital, Vol. 31, p. 28-62.

Behr, Andreas/Bellgardt, Egon (2000), Investitionsverhalten und Liquiditätsrestringiert-heit, Jahrbücher für Nationalökonomie und Statistik, Vol. 220, No. 3, p. 257-283.

Bernanke, Ben/Gertler, Mark (1990), Financial fragility and economic performance, Quarterly Journal of Economics, February, p. 87-114.

Bernanke, Ben/Gertler, Mark (1995), Inside the Black Box: The Credit Channel of Monetary Transmission, The Journal of Economic Perspectives, Vol. 9, Fall, p. 27-48.

Bernanke, Ben/Gertler, Mark/Gilchrist, Simon (1996), The Financial Accelerator and the Flight to Quality, The Review of Economics and Statistics, Vol. 78, February, p. 1-15.

Blanchard, Olivier J./Lopez-de-Silanes, Florencio/Shleifer, Andrei: What Do Firms with Cash Windfalls?, Journal of Financial Economics, Vol. 36, 1994, p. 337-360.

Blundell, Richard/Bond, Stephen (1998), Initial conditions and moment restrictions in dynamic panel data models, Journal of Econometrics 87, p. 115-143.

Blundell, Richard/Bond, Stephen/Devereux, Michael/Schiantarelli, Fabio (1992), Investement and Tobin's Q - Evidence from company panel data, Journal of Econometrics 51, p. 233-257.

Blundell, Richard/Bond, Stephen/Meghir, Costas (1995), Econometric Models of Company Investment, in Mátyás, L./Sevestre, P. (1995), p. 685-710.

Bond, Stephen/Meghir, Costas (1994): Dynamic Investment Models and the Firm´s Financial Policy, in: Review of Economic Studies, Vol. 61, p. 197-222.

Bontempi, Elena et. al. (2001), Capital Heterogeneity: Does it Matter? Fundamental *Q* and Investment on a Panel of Italian Firms, unpublished Working Paper.

Caballero, Ricardo J./Leahy, John V. (1996), Fixed Costs: The Demise of Marginal q, NBER Working Paper 5508, March 1996.

Cable, John (1985), Capital market information and industrial performance: The role of West German banks, The Economic Journal, Vol. 95, p. 118-132.

Chirinko, Robert S. (1993), Business Fixed Investment Spending: Modeling Strategies, Empirical Results, and Policy Implications, Journal of Economic Literature, Vol. XXXI, p. 1875-1911.

Chirinko, Robert S./Schaller, Huntley (1995), Why does liquidity matter in investment equations?, Journal of Money, Credit and Banking, Vol. 27, No.2, p. 527-548.

Chirinko, Robert S./Schaller, Huntley (1996), Bubbles, fundamentals and investment: A multiple equation testing strategy, Journal of Monetary Economics 38, p. 47-76.

Ciccolo, John/Fromm, Gary (1980), 'q', Corporate Investment, and Balance Sheet Behavior, Journal of Money , Credit, and Banking, Vol. 12, No. 2, p. 294-307.

Cuthbertson, K./Gasparro, D. (1995), Fixed Investment Decisions in UK Manufacturing: The Importance of Tobin´s Q, output and debt, European Economic Review, Vol. 39, p. 919-941.

Deutsche Bundesbank (1983): Abschlüsse der Unternehmen in der Bundesrepublik Deutschland 1965-1981, (Sonderdruck Nr. 5), 3. Auflage, Frankfurt am Main.

Deutsche Bundesbank (1989): Verhältniszahlen aus den Jahresabschlüssen der Unternehmen in der Bundesrepublik Deutschland für 1986, Frankfurt am Main.

Deutsche Bundesbank (1993): Jahresabschlüsse westdeutscher Unternehmen 1971 bis 1991, Frankfurt am Main.

Deutsche Bundesbank (1994): Verhältniszahlen aus Jahresabschlüssen westdeutscher Unternehmen für 1990, Frankfurt am Main.

Deutsche Bundesbank (1998a), The Methodological Basis of the Deutsche Bundesbank´s Corporate Balance Sheet Statistics, Monthly Report, October, p. 49-64.

Diamond, Douglas W. (1991), Monitoring and Reputation: The Choice between Bank Loans and Directly Placed Debt, The Journal of Political Economy, Vol. 29, No. 4, p. 689-721.

Elston, Julie Ann/Albach, Horst: Bank (1995), Affiliations and Firm Capital Investment in Germany, Ifo-Studien, Vol. 41, No. 1, p. 3-16.

Erickson, Timothy/Whited, Toni M. (2000a), Measurement Error and the Relationship between Investment and q, Journal of Political Economy, Vol. 108, No. 5, p. 1027-1057.

Erickson, Timothy/Whited, Toni M. (2000b), On the Information Content of Different Measures of Q, Unpublished Working Paper.

Fazzari, Steven M./Athey, Michael J. (1987), Asymmetric Information, Financing Constraints, and Investment, The Review of Economics and Statistics, Vol. 69, No. 3, p. 481-487.

Fazzari, Steven M./Hubbard, Glenn R./Petersen, Bruce C. (1996): Financing Constraints and Corporate Investment: Response to Kaplan and Zingales, NBER 5462, February 1996.

Fazzari, Steven M./Hubbard, Glenn R./ Petersen, Bruce C. (1988), Financing Constraints and Corporate Investment, Brookings Papers on Economic Activity, No. 1, p. 141-195.

Fazzari, Steven M./Hubbard, Glenn R./ Petersen, Bruce C. (2000), Investment-Cash Flow Sensitivities are Useful: A Comment on Kaplan and Zingales, The Quarterly Journal of Economics, Vol. 115, May, p. 695-705.

Gertler, Mark (1988), Financial Structure and Aggregate Economic Activity: An Overview, Journal of Money Credit and Banking, Vol. 20, No. 3, p. 559-596.

Gilchrist, Simon/Himmelberg, Charles P. (1995), Evidence on the Role of Cash Flow for Investment, Journal of Monetary Economics, Vol. 36, December, p. 541-572.

Gilchrist, Simon/Himmelberg, Charles P. (1998), Investment, Fundamental and Finance, NBER Working Paper 6652.

Hall, B. H./Cummins, C./Laderman, E. S./Mundy J. (1988), The R&D Masterfile Documentation, NBER Working Paper No. t00272.

Hansen, Gerd (2001): A bias-corrected least squares estimator of dynamic panel models, Allgemeines Statistisches Archiv, Vol. 85, p. 127-140.

Hayashi, Fumio (1982), Tobin's Marginal q and Average q: A Neoclassical Interpretation, Econometrica, Vol. 50, No. 1, p. 213-224.

Hayashi, Fumio (1997), The Main Bank System and Corporate Investment: An Empirical Reassessment, Unpublished Working Paper.

Holtz-Eakin, Douglas/Newey, Whitney/Rosen, Harvey S. (1988), Estimating Vector Autoregressions With Panel Data, Econometrica, Vol. 56, No. 6, p. 1371-1395.

Hoshi, Takeo/Kashyap, Anil/Scharfstein, David (1991), Corporate Structure, Liquidity, and Investment: Evidence from Japanese Industrial Groups, The Quarterly Journal of Economics, Vol. 106, p. 33-60.

Hu, Xiaoqiang/Schiantarelli, Fabio (1998): Investment and Capital Market Imperfections: A Switching Regression Approach Using U.S. Firm Panel Data, in: The Review of Economics and Statistics, Vol. LXXX, S. 466-479.

Hubbard, Glenn (1998), Capital-Market Imperfections and Investment, Journal of Economic Literature, Vol. 36, March, p. 193-225.

Hubbard, Glenn R./Kashyap, Anil K./Whited, Toni M. (1995), Internal Finance and Firm Investment, Journal of Money, Credit and Banking, Vol.27, No. 3, p. 683-701.

Jensen, Michael/Meckling, William H. (1976), Theory of the Firm: Managerial Behavior, Agency Costs and Ownership Structure, Journal of Financial Economics, Vol. 3, p. 305-360.

Jorgenson, Dale W. (1963), Capital Theory and Investment Behavior, American Economic Review, Vol. 53, No. 2, p. 247-259.

Jorgenson, Dale W. (1971): Econometric Studies of Investment Behaviour: A Survey, in: Journal of Economic Literature, Vol. IX, S. 1111-1147.

Judson, Ruth A./Owen Ann L. (1999), Estimating dynamic panel data models: a guide for macroeconomics, Economics Letters, Vol. 65, p. 9-15.

Kalckreuth, Ulf von (2001), The Monetary Transmission in Germany: New Perspectives on Financial Constraints and Investment Spending, Discussion Paper 19/01, Economic Research Centre of the Deutsche Bundesbank.

Kaplan, Steven N./Zingales, Luigi (1997), Do Investment-Cash Flow Sensitivities Provide Useful Measures of Financing Constraints?, Quarterly Journal of Economics, Vol. 112, February, p. 169-215.

Kaplan, Steven N./Zingales, Luigi (2000), Investment-Cash Flow Sensitivities are Not Valid Measures of Financing Constraints, Quarterly Journal of Economics, Vol. 115, May, p. 707-712.

Kiviet, Jan F. (1995): On bias, inconsistency and efficiency of various estimators in dynamic panel data models, Journal of Econometrics, Vol. 68, p. 53-78.

Klock, Mark/Thies, Clifford F./Baum, Christohper F. (1991), Tobin's q and Measurement Error: Caveat Investigator, Journal of Economics and Business, Vol. 43, p. 241-252.

Lamont, Owen (1997), Cash Flow and Investment: Evidence from internal Capital Markets, The Journal of Finance, Vol. 52, No. 1, p. 83-109.

Lang, Larry H.P./Stulz, Rene M./Walkling, Ralph A. (1991), A test of the free cash flow hypothesis, Journal of Financial Economics, Vol. 29, p. 315-335.

Lewellen, Wilbur G./Badrinath, S.G. (1997), On the measurement of Tobin's q, Journal of Financial Economics, Vol. 44, p. 77-122.

Lindenberg, Eric B./Ross, Stephen A. (1981), Tobin's q Ratio and Industrial Organization, Journal of Business, Vol. 54, p. 1-32.

Mátyás, L./Sevestre, P. (1995): The Econometrics of Panel Data, Dordrecht.

Mátyás, L. (ed.) (1999): Generalized Method of Moments Estimation, Cambridge University Press.

Mátyás, L./Harris D. (1999): Introduction to the Generalized Method of Moments Estimation, in: Mátyás, L. (ed.) (1999): Generalized Method of Moments Estimation, Cambridge University Press.

Meyer, John R./Kuh, Edwin (1957), The Investment Decision: An Empirical Study, Cambridge.

Minton, Bernadette/Schrand, Catherine (1999), The impact of cash flow voaltility on discretionary investment and the cost of debt and equity financing, Journal of Financial Economics, Vol. 54, p. 423-460.

Modigliani, Franco/Miller Merton H. (1958), The Cost of Capital, Corporation Finance and the Theory of Investment, American Economic Review, Vol. 48, No. 3, p. 261-297.

Myers, Stewart C. (1977), Determinants of Corporate Borrowing, Journal of Financial Economics, Vol. 5, p. 147-175.

Myers, Stewart C./Majluf, Nicholas (1984), Corporate Financing and Investment Decisions When Firms Have Information That Investors Do Not Have, Journal of Financial Economics, Vol. 13, No. 2, p. 187-221.

Ndikumana, Leonce (1999), Debt service, financing constraints, and fixed investment: evidence from panel data, Journal of Post Keynesian Economics, Vol. 21, Spring, No. 3, p. 455-478.

Nickell, Stephen (1981), Biases in Dynamic Models with Fixed Effects, Econometrica, Vol. 49, Issue 6, p. 1417-1426.

Oliner, Stephen D./Rudebusch, Glenn D. (1992): Sources of the Financing Hierarchy for Business Investment, in: The Review of Ecnomics and Statistics, Vol. LXXIV, S. 643-654.

Perfect, Steven B./Wiles, Kenneth, W. (1994), Alternative Constructions of Tobin´s q: An Empirical Comparison, Journal of Empirical Finance, Vol. 1, p. 313-341.

Salinger, Michael A./Summers, Lawrence H. (1983), Tax Reform and Corporate Investment: A Microeconometric Simulation Study, in: Feldstein, Martin S. (ed.) Behavioral Simulation Methods in Tax Policy Analysis, Chicago, p. 247-287.

Statistisches Bundesamt: Volkswirtschaftliche Gesamtrechnungen, Konten und Standardtabellen, Hauptbericht, (Fachserie 18, Reihe 1.3), verschiedene Jahrgänge, Stuttgart.

Stiglitz, Joseph E./Weiss, Andrew (1981), Credit Rationing in Markets with Imperfect Information, The American Economic Review, Vol. 71, No. 3, p. 393-410.

Stöss, Elmar (2001), Deutsche Bundesbank´s Corporate Balance Sheet Statistics and Areas of Application, Schmollers Jahrbuch, Vol. 121, Spring, p. 131-137.

Summers, Lawrence H. (1981), Taxation and Corporate Investment: A q-Theory Approach, Brookings Papers on Economic Activity, p. 67-127.

Taylor, John B. (1995), The Monetary Transmission Framework: An Empirical Framework, Journal of Economic Perspectives, Vol. 9, Fall, p. 11-26.

Thadden, Ernst-Ludwig von (1990), Bank Finance and Long-Term Investment, WWZ Discussion Papers, No. 9010.

Tobin, James (1969), A General Equilibrium Approach to Monetary Theory, Journal of Money, Credit, and Banking, Vol. 1, p. 15-29.

White, Halbert (1980), A Heteroskedasticity-Consistent Covariance Matrix Estimator and a Direct Test for Heteroskedasticity, in: Econometrica, Vol. 48, May 1980, p. 817-838.

Whited, Toni M. (1992), Debt, Liquidity Constraints, and Corporate Investment: Evidence from Panel Data, The Journal of Finance, Vol. XLVII, No. 4, p. 1425-1460.

Whited, Toni M. (1994), Problems with identifying adjustment costs from regressions of investment on q, Economics Letters, Vol. 46, p. 339-344.

Wildasin, David E. (1984), The q Theory of Investment with Many Capital Goods, The American Economic Review, Vol. 74, No. 1, p. 203-210.

Windmeijer, Frank (2000), A Finite Sample Correction for the Variance of Linear Two-Step GMM Estimators, IFS Working Paper 00/19.

Worthington, Paula R. (1992), Investment and market power, International Journal of Industrial Organization 10, p. 309-318.

Zhou, Chunsheng (2000), Time-To-Build and Investment, The Review of Economics and Statistics, Vol. 82, No. 2, p. 273-282.

GPSR Compliance

The European Union's (EU) General Product Safety Regulation (GPSR) is a set of rules that requires consumer products to be safe and our obligations to ensure this.

If you have any concerns about our products, you can contact us on ProductSafety@springernature.com

In case Publisher is established outside the EU, the EU authorized representative is:

Springer Nature Customer Service Center GmbH
Europaplatz 3
69115 Heidelberg, Germany

Batch number: 10725993

Printed by Printforce, the Netherlands